Positi~
to Rei~~~~ ~~~~~~ (every year)

365 + 1

**Pensamientos Positivos
para Reinventarse** (cada año)

**Pensées Positives
pour se Réinventer** (chaque année)

*Don't stop carving your own statue until it reveals
the divine splendor of your talents.*

*No pares de esculpir tu propia estatua hasta que descubras
el esplendor divino de tus talentos.*

*N' arrête pas de sculpter ta propre statue tant qu'elle n'aura pas révélé
la divine splendeur de tes talents.*

PLOTINUS (c205-c270) Alexandrian Philosopher

Edouard F. Lafontant / Master Motivator

insight
PUBLISHING GROUP
Tulsa, Oklahoma

365+1 POSITIVE THOUGHTS TO REINVENT YOURSELF
© 2005 by Edouard F. Lafontant

Published by Insight Publishing Group
8801 S. Yale, Suite 410
Tulsa, OK 74137
918-493-1718

ISBN 1-932503-35-8
Library of Congress catalog card number: 2004110580

Printed in the United States of America

To my beloved mother Simone
who gave me life,
To my sweet sister Simone
who is the joy of my life,
To my adorable wife Simone
who is the reason of my life.

A mi adorada madre Simone
que me ha dado la vida,
a mi querida hermana Simone
que es la alegría de mi vida,
a mi adorable esposa Simone
que es la razón de mi vida.

A ma mère adorée Simone
qui m'a donné la vie,
à ma très chère soeur Simone
qui est la joie de ma vie,
à mon adorable épouse Simone
qui est la raison de ma vie.

Preface

As the great philosopher Sophocles said, "A short saying oft contains much wisdom." This simple yet profound truth has proven itself time and time again throughout my personal life and professional career. I am a firm believer in the power of affirmation and a product of it, and I know from years of personal friendship and professional partnership with Edouard F. Lafontant that the same is true of him.

I first met Edouard more than thirty years ago when he became General Director of our partner company, Leadership Dynamics Institute, Inc., in Puerto Rico. Prior to joining my company (SMI), he worked as an accountant and manager at several government and private organizations. Edouard took to heart the many positive affirmations he had been recording since his teenage years and eventually became one of the most successful leaders in our business. In the past decades of his affiliation with SMI, he has impacted countless individuals in their quest for personal and professional success. I am proud to say that Edouard's successful career is one of my favorite success stories!

What you have in your hands is an invaluable compilation of quotations that Edouard has been gathering since his youth. Peter Hein of Denmark once said, "Brief sayings often open a small window on a large world." In this collection, philosophers, writers, civic and religious leaders, business experts, and Edouard as well, open small windows on large worlds of personal contentment and professional success.

My encouragement to you is to keep this book on your nightstand or dressing table. Read the quote for the day in the morning and again at night. An old Nordic adage states that "Brief sayings can often be read on two levels—superficial, entertaining and deeper, more profound." Read the quotations, take them to heart, and allow your mind to engage them on the deeper, more profound level. Let these truths transform your thinking into optimism, affirmation, and motivation to reinvent yourself and to meet your personal and professional goals.

Ralph Waldo Emerson, the great American philosopher and writer said, "Next to the originator of a good saying is the first quoter of it." Though I am not sure Edouard is necessarily the *first* quoter of many of these sayings, I for one am profoundly grateful he has compiled them (in three languages, no less!) in a format that can encourage and inspire readers around the world. And may I add another great quote, though I do not know who first said it:

God bless you!

Paul J. Meyer, Founder
Success Motivation® International, Inc.
The Meyer Family Enterprises
(more than 40 other companies)

Prefacio

Como dijo el gran filósofo Sófocles, "Un corto adagio a menudo contiene mucha sabiduría". Esta simple, sin embargo profunda verdad, ha sido convalidada una y otra vez a lo largo de mi vida tanto en lo personal como profesional. Creo firmemente en el poder de la afirmación y soy un producto de este método, y sé por mi amistad personal y por años de relaciones profesionales con Edouard F. Lafontant, él también piensa así.

Conocí a Edouard hace más de treinta años cuando se convirtió en Director General de nuestra compañía afiliada, Leadership Dynamics, en Puerto Rico. Antes de asociarse a Success Motivation® International, el trabajó con una agencia del gobierno americano en Haití y con algunas compañías privadas en Puerto Rico. Edouard hizo suyas las numerosas afirmaciones positivas que coleccionó desde su adolescencia y se convirtió eventualmente en uno de los más exitosos líderes de nuestro negocio. En los treinta y cinco años de su asociación con SMI, ha sido un factor determinante en la vida de un sinnúmero de individuos en su búsqueda de mayor éxito personal y profesional. Me siento orgulloso al decir que la carrera exitosa de Edouard es una de mis historias favoritas de éxito.

Lo que usted tiene en sus manos es una compilación invaluable de citaciones que Edouard ha reunido desde su juventud. Peter Hein de Dinamarca dijo una vez: "Los dichos cortos a menudo abren una pequeña ventana sobre un inmenso mundo". En esta colección, filósofos, escritores, líderes cívicos, religiosos y empresariales abren pequeñas ventanas sobre unos inmensos mundos de satisfacción personal y de éxito profesional.

Quiero alentarlo a mantener este libro en su mesa de noche, o en su tocador. Lea la citación del día por la mañana y otra vez por la noche. Como dice un antiguo refrán nórdico: "Una citación breve puede ser leída a menudo en dos niveles -

superficial, entretenida y profunda, más profunda". Lea estos pensamientos con mucha atención, hágalas suyas, y deje que su mente las absorba al nivel más profundo. Deje que estas verdades transformen su manera de pensar en una de optimismo, de afirmación y de motivación para reinventarse y lograr sus metas personales y profesionales.

Ralph Waldo Emerson, el gran filósofo y escritor americano dijo: "Al lado del creador de un buen refrán se situa el primero que lo cita". Aunque no estoy seguro que Edouard sea necesariamente el *primero* que haya repetido muchas de estas citas, por mi parte me siento profundamente agradecido que él las haya recopilado (en tres idiomas) en un formato que puede alentar e inspirar a lectores alrededor del mundo. Permítame añadir otra gran cita, aunque no sepa quién lo dijo primero:

¡Dios te bendiga!

Paul J. Meyer
Fundador de Success Motivation® International, Inc. y Las Empresas de la Familia Meyer
(más de 40 otras empresas)

Preface

«Un proverbe contient souvent beaucoup de sagesse,» a dit Sophocle, le grand philosophe. Cette simple mais profonde vérité, je l'ai vécue en maintes occasions dans ma vie privée et au cours de ma carrière professionnelle. Je crois fermement en la force inspiratrice des maximes et leur sagesse est mon guide. Edouard Lafontant appartient à la même école; de nombreuses années d'amitié et de coopération professionnelle me permettent de l'affirmer.

J'ai rencontré Edouard pour la première fois, il y a de cela plus de trente ans, quand il est devenu Président-Directeur Général de la "Leadership Dynamics Institute", filliale portoricaine de notre compagnie "Success Motivation® International (SMI)." Avant de se joindre à notre organization, il a travaillé dans une Agence du Gouvernement Américain et dans plusieurs compagnies privées. Edouard a toujours mis en pratique les nombreuses pensées positives qu'il n'a jamais cessé de compiler depuis son adolescence; aussi, est-il devenu un des plus brillants leaders de notre entreprise. Durant les trente cinq ans de son affiliation à la SMI, il a exercé une influence marquante sur un nombre incalculable d'individus en quête de succès dans leur vie privée et dans leur carrière professionnelle. Je suis fier d'ajouter que la carrière exemplaire d'Edouard figure parmi mes histoires de réussites professionnelles préférées!

Ce livre que vous avez en votre possession est une sélection de pensées d'une valeur inestimable qu'Edouard n'a pas cessé de compiler depuis son adolescence. Comme a dit un penseur danois, Peter Hein, «Souvent de simples proverbes ouvrent une petite fenêtre sur un monde immense». Dans cette compilation de pensées positives, des philosophes, des écrivains, des leaders politiques ou religieux, des hommes d'affaires célèbres et Edouard Lafontant lui-même ouvrent de petites fenêtres sur de vastes horizons de satisfaction personnelle et de réussites professionnelles.

Je vous encourage à faire de cet ouvrage votre livre de chevet. Lisez la pensée du jour, le matin à votre réveil et le soir avant de dormir. D'après un vieil adage scandinave «Les proverbes paraissent amusants après une lecture superficielle mais profonds quand on y réfléchit.» Lisez ces pensées avec attention, prenez les à coeur et permettez à votre esprit d'en dégager la force positive et la sagesse profonde. Laissez ces vérités transformer vos réflexions en optimisme, en conviction et en motivation pour vous réinventer et atteindre les objectifs de votre vie privée et de votre carrière.

Ralph Waldo Emerson, le grand philosophe et écrivain américain a dit: «Tout de suite après l'auteur d'un bon mot se classe celui qui le premier le cite.» Je doute qu'Edouard soit le *premier* à citer beaucoup de ces pensées, cependant je lui sais infiniment gré de les avoir compilées en trois langues dans un format qui peut encourager et inspirer les lecteurs à travers le monde. Puis-je ajouter une magnifique citation dont j'ignore l'auteur:

Que Dieu vous bénisse!

Paul J. Meyer, Fondateur
Success Motivation® International, Inc. et
Les Entreprises de la Famille Meyer
(plus 40 autres compagnies)

Acknowledgements

I wish to express my thanks and my gratitude to all the women and men whose dedication and enthusiasm made this book a reality:

Paul J. Meyer, my mentor, instilled into me his immense optimism and encouraged me since the inception of the project. He also suggested the biblical quotes.

Dr. Barbara Chesser has edited the English version and suggested many pertinent modifications all along the process.

Albert Héraux, my longtime friend, revised the French and the English versions to make them simpler and more precise.

My daughter Dominique and my son Edouard, Jr., revised the Spanish version to enhance the latin flavor.

Dr. Henri Labrousse, my brother-in-law, of Sherbrooke, Canada, made the final revision of the French version to eliminate the slightest errors of translation and composition.

Eng. Abelardo Maldonado, my Mexican fellow motivator graciously permitted us to use the wonderful logo of his company "Man Sculpting His Own Statue" as the cover photo of this book.

Ralph De Pas of New York, my cousin, photographed this sculpture for the cover.

The team of Leadership Dynamics: Alba Berríos, María Mercedes Millán, Sonia Meléndez, Héctor Aponte and Carmen C. Portugués handled with efficiency, enthusiasm, and patience the many details of the administrative aspect of this project.

My friends in Puerto Rico and elsewhere: Jacques Faubert, Victor Cassagnol, Frédérique Clermont, Jacques Aimé, Mireille Gaëtjens, Anne & Alain Dresse, Pilar & Philippe Scott always encouraged me with their valuable suggestions and their eagerness to see the book completed.

Simone, my dear wife, whose love is for me an inexhaustible source of inspiration and strength.

John Mason, Denise Dietz and the staff at Insight Publishing for their professionalism and creativity.

And the authors of these thoughts whose wisdom so significantly influenced my personal life.

Agradecimientos

Quiero expresar mi agradecimiento y mi gratitud a todas las personas cuya dedicación y entusiasmo hicieron posible la publicación de este libro:

Paul J. Meyer, mi mentor, me comunicó su inmenso optimismo y me alentó desde el principio. También me sugirió las citas bíblicas.

La Doctora Bárbara Chesser revisó la versión inglesa y sugirió muchas modificaciones pertinentes a lo largo del proceso.

Albert Héraux, mi amigo de siempre, revisó la versión francesa y la versión inglesa para una mayor simplificación y precisión.

Mi hija Dominique y mi hijo Edouard, Jr. se encargaron de la revisión de la versión del español para preservar su sabor latino.

El Dr. Henri Labrousse, mi cuñado de Sherbrooke, Canada, revisó la versión francesa final para eliminar los errores de traducción y de redacción.

El Ing. Abelardo Maldonado, mi colega mejicano, que graciosamente me ha permitido utilizar el admirable logo de su empresa "El hombre esculpiendo su propia estatua" cuya foto adorna la portada del libro. Esta foto fue tomada por Ralph De Pas, mi primo de Nueva York.

El equipo de Leadership Dynamics, mis ayudantes, Alba Berríos, María Mercedes Millán, Sonia Meléndez, Héctor Aponte y Carmen C. Portugués coordinaron con gran entusiasmo y una paciencia a toda prueba los numerosos detalles de la gestión del proyecto.

Mis amigos y amigas de Puerto Rico y de la diáspora Jacques Faubert, Victor Cassagnol, Frédérique Clermont, Jacques Aimé, Mireille Gaëtjens, Anne & Alain Dresse, Pilar & Philippe Scott siempre me alentaron con su generosa contribución y su anhelo de ver el libro terminado.

Simone, mi queridísima esposa, cuyo amor es para mí una fuente inagotable de inspiración y de energía.

John Mason, Denise Dietz y el equipo de Insight Publishing por su profesionalismo y su creatividad.

Y los autores de esos pensamientos cuya sabiduría ha marcado de manera tan significativa mi vida personal.

Remerciements

Je tiens à exprimer mes remerciements et ma gratitude à toutes celles et tous ceux qui, par leur dévouement et leur enthousiasme, ont rendu possible la publication de cet ouvrage:

Paul J. Meyer, mon mentor, m'a communiqué son immense optimisme et m'a encouragé dès le début du projet. Il a aussi suggéré les citations bibliques.

Dr. Barbara Chesser a révise la version anglaise et suggéré des modifications pertinentes tout au along du processus.

Albert Héraux, mon ami de toujours, a révise la version française et la version anglaise pour les rendre plus simples et plus précises.

Ma fille Dominique et mon fils Edouard Jr. ont révise la version espagnole pour en préserver la saveur latine.

Le Dr. Henri Labrousse, mon beau-frère de Sherbrooke, Canada, a révise la version française finale pour en éliminer les moindres erreurs de traduction et de rédaction.

Abelardo Maldonado, mon confrère mexicain, m'a gracieusement permis d'utiliser l'admirable logo de sa compagnie «L'Homme sculptant sa propre statue» qui illustre la couverture du livre.

Ralph De Pas, mon cousin de New York, a photographié cette statue pour la couverture.

L'équipe de Leadership Dynamics, Alba Berríos, María Mercedes Millán, Sonia Meléndez, Héctor Aponte et Carmen C. Portugués, a coordonné avec enthousiasme et patience les nombreux détails de la gestion de ce projet.

Mes amis de Porto Rico et de la diaspora: Jacques Faubert, Victor Cassagnol, Frédérique Clermont, Jacques Aimé, Mireille Gaëtjens, Anne et Alain Dresse, Pilar et Philippe Scott m'ont toujours encouragé par leurs suggestions heureuses et leur empressement de voir enfin achevé le livre.

Simone, ma très chère épouse, dont l'amour est pour moi une source intarissable d'inspiration et d'énergie.

John Mason, à Denise Dietz et à toute l'equipe de Insight Publishing pour leur professionalisme et leur créativité.

Et les auteurs de ces pensées dont la sagesse a si profondément marqué ma vie personnelle.

Introduction

This book is a selection of positive thoughts compiled in the course of many years. I loved reading quotes, they reflect the essence of their author's thinking and they are for me a precious source of inspiration and motivation.

I remember, on the last day of high school, the teacher asked the students which motto they elected to inspire them in life. I, already "a man of quotes," spontaneously responded, "Mens agitat molem" (Spirit animates matter.) This motto still motivates me and I often use it in our personal motivation seminars to stimulate the participants.

I must admit that when I started this compilation, it was not restricted to positive thoughts. It included any interesting thought from my readings and my own ones from daily observations patiently recorded in an elegant notebook I bought at the mature age of fourteen. The first entry was: "What I expect from life? Death." Thanks God, I have improved since!

My affiliation with the Success Motivation® International, Inc. companies, founded by Paul J. Meyer, has strengthened my enthusiasm in the pursuit of this endeavour. From my reading of the book by Og Mandino, *The Greatest Salesman in the World,* I keep in my memory with a special fervor the title of the fifth scroll: "I will live this day as if it was my last and my last will be my best." In 1999 I contacted Mr. Sherman Wildman, owner of the WOSO Radio Station in San Juan, Puerto Rico, and offered to broadcast daily a positive quote to cheer up the audience and prepare it for the new challenges of the coming millennium. He accepted gracefully and suggested that I read them in Spanish and in English. This program was very successful. From the first days of the program, I started feeling the benefits of these positive thoughts in my personal life, in conversations with friends and clients, in my facilitation work, and public speaking. Then gradually, I realized that many people could benefit from the wisdom of these exciting positive thoughts. So I decided to have them published in three languages under the same cover to motivate and inspire as large a public as possible.

Many books of quotes have been published without any special emphasis; but *365+1 Positive Thoughts to Reinvent Yourself (every year)* focuses on positive thoughts. And this is my contribution! This quote from Ralph Waldo Emerson, "Thoughts rule the world," convinces me that positive thoughts will help build a better and more positive world.

Loren Eiseley in his book, *The Young Man and the Starfish*, wrote this wonderful story:

A wise man was taking a sunrise walk along the beach. In the distance he caught sight of a young man who seemed to be dancing along the waves. As he got closer he saw that the young man was picking up starfish from the sand and tossing them gently back into the ocean.

"What are you doing?" the wise man asked.

"The sun is coming up and the tide is going out; if I don't throw them in they'll die."

"But young man, there are miles and miles of beach with starfish all along it—you can't possibly make a difference."

The young man bent down, picked up another starfish, and threw it lovingly back into the ocean, past the breaking waves. "It made a difference for that one," he replied.

If every day, you read one of these positive thoughts, your brain will receive a positive impact; it is like hammering on your chisel to "carve your own statue." At the end of the year your brain will receive 365 impacts—even 366—which provoke a tremendous positive change in you, just like the sculptor who with each stroke finds himself closer to what he visualized his work to be. Reading this book will make a difference, maybe a big difference.

Now, if you repeat this experience every year, you will have the wonderful feeling of discovering a deeper meaning in each quote. It is the same thought, the same words, but your mental attitude will have changed. If you think that you have completed the work of shaping your own statue, the finishing process will not end until it reveals to you the "divine splendor of your talents."

I sincerely hope you make it happen. Happy sculpting!

Edouard F. Lafontant
San Juan, Puerto Rico
Spring 2004

Introducción

Este libro es una extraordinaria colección de pensamientos positivos que he reunido a lo largo de los años. Siempre me ha gustado leer las citas porque engloban las más finas y sustanciales expresiones de sus autores y siempre han constituido para mí una fuente de inspiración y motivación.

Me acuerdo en el último día de clase el maestro pidió a los alumnos escoger un pensamiento que les guiara a lo largo de sus vidas. Yo, un amante de las citas, respondí "Mens agitat molem", ("El espíritu mueve la materia"). Este pensamiento aún me motiva y lo cito a menudo durante mis seminarios de motivación personal para alentar a los participantes.

Tengo que admitir que al principio, mi colección no era necesariamente de pensamientos positivos. Recuerdo que a los 14 años, compré una bonita libreta para escribir todas las citas interesantes que encontraba en mis lecturas y mis observaciones personales y lo primero que escribí fue: "Lo que espero de la vida: La muerte". ¡Gracias a Dios, he mejorado desde entonces!

Mi asociación con el Sr. Paul J. Meyer, fundador del conglomerado de las compañías de SUCCESS MOTIVATION INSTITUTE ha estimulado aún más mi interés en este empeño. Siempre me ha gustado el título del quinto pergamino del libro de Og Mandino, *El vendedor más grande del mundo:* "Viviré este día como si fuese mi último y mi último será mi mejor". Así en el 1999, ya que este año era el último del milenio, fui a ver a mi amigo el Sr. Sherman Wildman, dueño de la Estación de Radio-difusión WOSO en San Juan de Puerto Rico para compartir la idea de ofrecer diariamente un mensaje positivo para animar a su audiencia y preparar a la gente para encarar valientemente los retos del nuevo milenio. Mr. Wildman aceptó mi oferta y ya estaba yo encaminado a escoger 365 + 1 pensamientos positivos y sugirió leerlos en inglés y español. El programa fue un gran éxito.

Día a día podría apreciar el efecto que estos pensamientos tenían en mi vida, mi conversación con amigos y clientes, en mis reuniones de facilitador y mis conferencias. Entonces, me convencí que muchas otras personas podrían disfrutar de la sabiduría de estos maravillosos pensamientos y decidí preparar este libro en tres idiomas para inspirar y motivar a tantas personas como fuera posible.

Muchas excelentes obras de pensamientos han sido publicadas dirigidas a todos los aspectos de la vida; sin embargo *365 + 1 Pensamientos Positivivos para Reinventarse (cada año)* contiene solamente pensamientos positivos y eso es mi contribución especial a este campo.

Ralph Waldo Emerson decía "Los pensamientos gobiernan al mundo". Estoy más que nunca convencido y creo que las ideas positivas ayudarán a construir un mundo más positivo.

Loren Eisenley en su libro *El Joven y la Estrella de Mar,* escribió esta preciosa historia:

Un sabio estaba paseando al amanecer en una playa. En la distancia divisó una persona que parecía estaba bailando a lo largo de la playa. Al acercarse vió un joven que recogía unas estrellas de mar y gentilmente las devolvía al agua.

"¿Qué estás haciendo?" le preguntó el sabio.

"El sol sale pronto y la marea baja, si yo no las devuelvo al agua, morirán".

"Pero, joven, hay millas y millas de playa cubiertas de estrellas de mar, ¿qué diferencia puede haber?"

El joven recogió otra estrella y la lanzó al mar mientras contestaba: "Para ésta habrá una diferencia".

Cada día, cada vez que usted lea uno de estos pensamientos, su cerebro recibe un impacto positivo. Es como el golpe de martillo sobre el cincel para "esculpir su propia estatua". Al final del año su mente habrá recibido 365 impactos – hasta 366 – lo que provoca un tremendo cambio positivo en usted, igual que el escultor con cada golpe se acerca más a lo que ha visualizado que sea su obra. Obviamente, habrá una diferencia y posiblemente una inmensa diferencia.

Y si usted lo hace cada año, tendrá una maravillosa experiencia al percibir un sentido un tanto diferente en cada cita. Es el mismo pensamiento, las mismas palabras, pero es usted el que ha cambiado su actitud y si cree que ha completado su trabajo y que ha esculpido su estatua a su gusto, tendrá que seguir puliéndola todos los días hasta que le revele "el esplendor divino de sus talentos".

Sinceramente espero que se cumpla este deseo suyo. ¡Adelante!

Edouard F. Lafontant
San Juan, Puerto Rico
Primavera 2004

Introduction

Ce livre est une sélection de pensées positives compilées durant de nombreuses années. J'ai toujours aimé les maximes, elles contiennent, pour ainsi dire, la «substantifique moelle» des écrits de leur auteur et ont toujours constitué pour moi une source d'inspiration et de motivation.

Je me souviens de ce dernier jour de classe où l'instituteur demanda aux élèves quelle maxime ils avaient choisie pour les guider dans la vie. Moi, déjà amateur de maximes, répondis «Mens agitat molem», (C'est l'esprit qui anime la matière.) Cette maxime me motive encore et je la cite souvent dans mes séminaires de motivation personnelle pour stimuler les participants.

Au début, cette compilation ne contenait pas uniquement des pensées positives. Dans un élégant carnet acheté à l'âge «mûr» de quatorze ans, je notais soigneusement toutes les maximes qui me frappaient et ausi mes réflexions personnelles. La première maxime notée dans ce précieux carnet! «Ce que j'attends de la vie? La mort.» Je ne pense plus de cette façon, Dieu merci!

Mon affiliation aux compagnies de la Success Motivation Institute fondées par Mr. Paul J. Meyer a stimulé mon enthousiasme dans l'accomplissement de cette tâche.

Je garderai toujours dans ma mémoire, avec une ferveur spéciale, le titre du cinquième chapitre du livre de Og Mandino, *Le plus grand vendeur du monde;* je cite «Je vivrai ce jour comme s'il était le dernier, et mon dernier sera le meilleur.» En 1999, je proposai à Mr. Sherman Wildman, propriétaire de la station de radio WOSO de San Juan, Porto Rico la lecture quotidienne d'une pensée positive pour stimuler les auditeurs et les préparer à faire face aux nouveaux défis du millénaire qui approchait. Il accepta l'idée avec enthousiasme et me demanda de lire les pensées en espagnol et en anglais. Le programme fut un succès.

Au fil des jours, je pouvais vérifier les effets bénéfiques de ces pensées positives dans ma vie personnelle, dans mes rapports avec mes amis et mes clients et dans mon travail. Alors, comprenant que beaucoup d'autres personnes pourraient profiter de la sagesse de ces merveilleuses pensées positives, j'ai décidé d'écrire ce livre en trois langues pour inspirer et motiver autant de personnes que possible.

Beaucoup d'excellents ouvrages sur les maximes, qui s'adressent à tous les aspects de la vie en général, ont été publiés; cependant, *365 + 1 Pensées positives pour vous réinventer (chaque année)* a la particularité de ne contenir que des pensées positives. Telle est ma contribution dans ce domaine!

Selon Ralph Waldo Emerson, «Les maximes mènent le monde,» plus que jamais, j'en suis convaincu. Les pensées positives aideront à construire un monde meilleur et plus positif.

Loren Eiseley, dans son livre, *The young man and the starfish.* (Le jeune homme et l'étoile de mer) raconte cette merveilleuse histoire:

Un vieil homme, au lever du jour, se promenait sur une plage. De loin, un jeune homme qui paraissait danser au long des vagues attira son attention. En s'approchant de plus près, il vit que le jeune homme ramassait des étoiles de mer sur le sable pour les remettre avec soin dans la mer.

-Que fais-tu, jeune homme?, demanda le vieil homme.

-Le soleil se lève et la marée baisse, si je ne les retourne pas à la mer, elles périront.

-Mais, jeune homme, il y a des milliers de kilomètres de sable et autant d'étoiles de mer dans cette situation ¡Tes efforts ne feront aucune difference!

Le jeune homme se baissa, ramassa une autre étoile de mer et la déposa avec délicatesse dans l'océan, au delà des vagues.

-Pour celle là, répondit le jeune homme, cela fait une différence!

Chaque jour et chaque fois que vous lisez une pensée positive, votre cerveau reçoit un impact. C'est un coup de marteau sur votre burin pour sculpter votre propre statue. À la fin de l'année, votre cerveau aura reçu 365 impacts et même 366, ce qui provoquera en vous un changement positif remarquable pareil à celui du sculpteur qui, à chaque coup de marteau, se retrouve plus près de l'oeuvre qu'il a visualisée. Certainement, la lecture de ce livre fera une différence, une différence marquante!

Si vous lisez ces pensées, chaque jour chaque année, vous aurez la merveilleuse sensation de découvrir un sens plus profond dans chaque pensée. Ce sera la même pensée, les mêmes mots, mais votre attitude mentale aura changé. Attention, même si vous croyez avoir achevé de sculpter votre propre statue, sachez que l'oeuvre ne sera pas complète tant qu'elle ne vous aura pas révélé "la divine splendeur de vos talents."

Je vous le souhaite sincèrement. Bonne besogne!

Edouard F. Lafontant
San Juan, Porto Rico
Printemps 2004

JANUARY—ENERO—JANVIER

1 ....PAUL J. MEYER
2 ....RALPH WALDO EMERSON
3 ....VICTOR EMIL FRANKL

4 ....MORTIMER J. ADLER
5 ....VICTOR HUGO
6 ....SAN JUAN DE LA CRUZ

7 ....JIDDU KRISHNAMURTI
8 ....JAMES ALLEN
9 ....ROBERT L. STEVENSON

10 ....ELEANOR ROOSEVELT
11 ....EUGENIO MARÍA DE HOSTOS
12 ....THE BIBLE

13 ....A. DE ST. EXUPÉRY
14 ....JAPANESE PROVERB
15 ....MARTIN LUTHER KING JR.

16 ....LEONARDO DA VINCI
17 ....MENG-TSE
18 ....BOOKER T. WASHINGTON

19 ....DOROTHY PARKER
20 ....KONRAD ADENAUER
21 ....PIERRE E. TRUDEAU

22 ....COLIN POWELL
23 ....HENRY BROOKS ADAMS
24 ....MENANDER

25 ....HERACLITUS
26 ....EDOUARD F. LAFONTANT
27 ....MOTHER THERESA OF CALCUTTA

28 ....LAO-TZU
29 ....FRANZ KAFKA
30 ....THOMAS JEFFERSON

31 ....ROBERT MILLIKAN

January 1
1 de enero
1ᵉʳ janvier

Whatever you vividly imagine, ardently desire, sincerely believe, and enthusiastically act upon . . . must inevitably come to pass!

❧☙

Todo lo que vívidamente imaginamos, ardientemente deseamos, sinceramente creemos y emprendemos con entusiasmo, inevitablemente sucederá.

❧☙

Tout ce que vous imaginez vivement, désirez ardemment, croyez sincèrement et pour quoi vous travaillez avec enthousiasme, se réalisera inévitablement.

PAUL J. MEYER (b. 1928)

American Entrepreneur & Educator
Founder of the Success Motivation Institute companies
Empresario & Educador Americano
Fundador de las Empresas Success Motivation Institute
Homme d'affaires et éducateur américain
Fondateur des entreprises Success Motivation Institute

WHAT IS SUCCESS?

To laugh often and much;
To win the respect of intelligent people
And the affection of children;
To earn the appreciation of honest critics
And endure the betrayal of false friends;
To appreciate beauty;
to find the best in others;
to leave the world a bit better
whether by a healthy child,
a garden patch or a redeemed social condition;
to know even one life has breathed
easier because you have lived;
this is to have SUCCEEDED.

RALPH WALDO EMERSON (1803-1882)

American Philosopher, Poet & Essayist

2 *de enero*

¿QUÉ ES ÉXITO?

Reir a menudo y mucho;
Ganar el respeto de las personas inteligentes
Y el afecto de los niños;
Ganar el aprecio de los críticos honestos
Y soportar la traición de los falsos amigos,
Apreciar la belleza;
Encontrar lo mejor en la gente,
Dejar el mundo un poco mejor,
O sea, con un niño saludable
O un pequeño jardín
O una condición social mejorada;
Saber que por lo menos una criatura
Ha vivido mejor gracias a nuestro paso por la tierra
Eso es haber tenido EXITO.

RALPH WALDO EMERSON (1803-1882)

Filósofo, Poeta & Ensayista Americano

LA RÉUSSITE, C'EST QUOI?

Rire souvent et à gorge deployée
Gagner le respect des gens intelligents
Et l'affection des enfants;
Mériter l'attention des critiques honnêtes
Et endurer la trahison des faux amis;
Apprécier la beauté;
Découvrir le meilleur chez les autres;
Laisser le monde un peu mieux
Soit avec un enfant sain, un petit jardin
Ou une situation sociale injuste redressée.
Savoir que même une seule créature
A mieux vécu grâce à votre passage sur terre
C'est ça la réussite.

RALPH WALDO EMERSON (1803-1882)

Philosophe, poète et essayiste américain

January 3
3 de enero
3 janvier

Living is an art. It is the most difficult and complex art to be practiced by mankind. It does not consist of doing this or that in particular; it is living fully in transforming oneself in what one potentially can become. In the art of living, one is both the artist and the subject of one's art, the sculptor and the marble, the physician and the patient.

ഇൗരു

Vivir es un arte. Es el arte más difícil y complejo a ser practicado por el hombre. El arte de vivir no consiste en hacer tal o cual cosa en particular, sino el vivir en sí, el convertirse en lo que uno potencialmente es. En el arte de vivir uno es ambas cosas, el artista y el objeto de su arte. Es el escultor y el mármol, el médico y el paciente.

ഇൗരു

Vivre est un art. C'est l'art le plus difficile et le plus complexe à pratiquer par le genre humain. L'art de vivre ne consiste pas à faire telle chose ou telle autre, mais plutôt en une réflexion constante sur l'immensité de notre potentiel. Dans l'art de vivre on est à la fois l'artiste et le sujet de son art, le sculpteur et le marbre, le médecin et le patient.

VICTOR EMIL FRANKL (1905-1997)

Austrian Psychologist, Author of *The Will to Meaning*
Psicólogo Austriaco, Autor de *The Will to Meaning*
Psychologue autrichien, auteur de *The Will to Meaning*

In Aristotelian terms, the good leader must have *ethos*, *pathos* and *logos*. The *ethos* is his moral character, the source of his ability to persuade. The *pathos* is his ability to touch feelings, to move people emotionally. The *logos* is his ability to give solid reasons for action, to move people intellectually.

೩೦೮೩

Según Aristóteles, el buen liderato se compone de *ethos*, *pathos* y *logos*. El *ethos* representa su carácter moral, fuente de toda habilidad para persuadir. *Pathos* es la habilidad de estimular las emociones o motivar emocionalmente. *Logos* es la habilidad de dar buenas razones para la acción o motivar intelectualmente.

೩೦೮೩

Selon Aristote, le bon leader se caractérise par l'*ethos*, le *pathos* et le *logos*. L'*ethos* est sa force morale et son pouvoir de persuasion. Le *pathos* est son habileté à réveiller les émotions et à attendrir; le *logos* son habileté à inspirer aux autres de solides raisons d'agir et à stimuler leur intelligence.

MORTIMER J. ADLER (1902-2001)

American Philosopher & Educator
Filósofo & Educador Americano
Philosophe et éducateur américain

January 5
5 de enero
5 janvier

The future has several names.
For the weak, it is the UNATTAINABLE.
For the timid, it is the UNKNOWN.
For the brave, it is OPPORTUNITY.

૪૭૯૩

El futuro tiene varios nombres.
Para los débiles, es el INACCESIBLE.
Para los tímidos, es el DESCONOCIDO.
Para los valientes, es la OPORTUNIDAD.

૪૭૯૩

Le futur a plusieurs noms.
Pour les faibles, c'est L'INACCESSIBLE.
Pour les timides, c'est L'INCONNU.
Pour les braves, c'est L'OPPORTUNITÉ.

VICTOR HUGO (1802-1885)

French Writer
Escritor Francés
Écrivain français

The purpose of education is not to prepare youngsters for professions but to temper their soul for the challenges of life.

ഊരു

El propósito de la educación no es preparar a los jóvenes para las profesiones, sino templar el alma para la vida.

ഊരു

Le but de l'éducation n'est pas de préparer les jeunes pour les professions, mais de façonner leur âme pour les défis de la vie.

SAN JUAN DE LA CRUZ (1542-1591)

Spanish Carmelite Mystic
Místico Carmelita Español
Mystique carmélite espagnol

January 7
07 de enero
07 janvier

In oneself lies the whole world, and if you know how to look and learn, then the door is there and the key is in your hand. Nobody on earth but yourself can give you either the key or the door to open.

ॐ

Dentro de nosotros se encuentra el mundo entero y si usted sabe cómo buscar y aprender, entonces la puerta está ahí y la llave está en su mano. Nadie en el mundo puede darle la llave o la puerta para abrir, sino usted mismo.

ॐ

Le monde entier se trouve en nous-mêmes et si nous savons comment chercher et apprendre, la porte est là et la clef est dans notre main. Personne ne peut nous donner ni la clef ni la porte à ouvrir.

JIDDU KRISHNAMURTI (1895-1986)

Indian Philosopher
Filósofo Indio
Philosophe indien

A man is literally *what he thinks;* his character being the complete sum of all his thoughts.

&OCB

Un hombre es literalmente *lo que piensa,* siendo su carácter la suma de sus pensamientos.

&OCB

Un homme est littéralement *ce qu'il pense,* sa personnalité étant la somme de ses pensées.

JAMES ALLEN (1864-1912)

English Writer, Author of the book *As a Man Thinketh*
Escritor Inglés, Autor del libro *As a Man Thinketh*
Écrivain anglais, auteur du livre *As a Man Thinketh*

January 9
9 de enero
9 janvier

A goal in life is the unique fortune to look for; but don't look for it in foreign places but in your own heart.

ৡ০03

Una meta en la vida es la única fortuna digna de ser buscada, y no se debe buscar en tierras extrañas, sino en el propio corazón.

ৡ০03

Avoir un but dans la vie est l'unique richesse à convoiter, mais il ne faut pas le chercher ailleurs que dans son coeur.

ROBERT LOUIS STEVENSON (1850-1894)

British Writer
Escritor Británico
Écrivain britannique

January 10
10 de enero
10 janvier

You gain strength, courage and confidence by every experience
in which you really stop to look fear in the face . . . You must do
the thing which you think you cannot do.

೫೦೦೩

Usted adquiere fortaleza, coraje y confianza con cada
experiencia cuando usted realmente se detiene a mirar el miedo
cara a cara. Usted tiene que hacer lo que piensa que no puede
hacer.

೫೦೦೩

Vous devenez plus fort, plus courageux et plus sûr de vous-même
chaque fois que vous acceptez de confronter la peur. Faites
toujours ce qui paraît dépasser votre compétence.

ELEANOR ROOSEVELT (1884-1962)

Diplomat, Humanitarian
Wife of 32nd President of the United States of America
Diplomática, Humanista
Esposa del 32° Presidente de los Estados Unidos de América
Diplomate, humaniste
Épouse du 32e Président des États-Unis d'Amérique

It is in our heart that the revolution shall be made.

৪৩০৫৪

La revolución hay que hacerla en el corazón de los hombres.

৪৩০৫৪

C'est dans le coeur des hommes que la révolution doit se faire.

EUGENIO MARÍA DE HOSTOS (1839-1903)

Puerto Rican Educator, Writer & Journalist
Educador, Escritor & Periodista Puertorriqueño
Éducateur, écrivain et journaliste portoricain

January 12
12 de enero
12 janvier

The first of all the commandments is to love the Lord your God with all your heart, and with all your soul, and with all your mind, and with all your strength. And the second commandment is to love your neighbor as yourself.

&⊃⊂&

El primer mandamiento es: Al Señor tu Dios amarás con todo tu corazón, con toda tu alma, con toda tu inteligencia y con todas tus fuerzas. Y después viene éste: Amarás a tu prójimo como a tí mismo.

&⊃⊂&

Le premier commandement: . . . tu aimeras le Seigneur ton Dieu de tout ton coeur, de toute ton âme, de tout ton esprit et de toutes tes forces. Le second: Tu aimeras ton prochain comme toi-même.

THE BIBLE — LA BIBLIA — LA BIBLE

St. Mark 12:30-31
San Marcos 12:30-31
Saint Marc 12:30-31

January 13
13 de enero
13 janvier

It is only with the heart that one completely can see. The essence of things cannot be seen with the eyes.

ॐ౧౧

Se ve bien solamente con el corazón. Lo esencial no se puede ver con los ojos.

ॐ౧౧

On ne voit bien qu'avec le coeur. L'essentiel est invisible pour les yeux.

ANTOINE DE ST. EXUPÉRY (1900-1944)

French Aviator & Writer
Aviador & Escritor Francés
Aviateur et écrivain français

Vision without action is daydream. Action without vision is a nightmare.

❧⟩⟨❧

Visión sin acción es soñar despierto. Acción sin visión es una pesadilla.

❧⟩⟨❧

Une vision sans action est un fantasme. Une action sans vision, un cauchemar.

JAPANESE PROVERB
PROVERBIO JAPONES
PROVERBE JAPONAIS

January 15
15 de enero
15 janvier

Everybody can be great, because anybody can serve. You don't have to have a college degree to serve. You don't have to make your subject and your verb agree to serve. You don't have to know Plato and Aristotle to serve. You don't have to know Einstein's Theory of Relativity to serve. You don't have to know the second theory of the thermo-dynamics in physics to serve. You only need a heart full of grace. A soul generated by love.

෨෦ඏ

Cada uno de nosotros puede ser grande, porque cada uno puede servir a los demás. Usted no tiene que tener un grado universitario para servir. Usted no tiene que conjugar su sujeto con su verbo para servir. Usted no necesita conocer de Platón y Aristóteles para servir. Usted no tiene que conocer la Teoría de la Relatividad de Einstein para servir. Usted no tiene que saber de la segunda teoría de la termodinámica en la física para servir. Usted solamente necesita un corazón lleno de gracia y un alma inspirada por el amor.

෨෦ඏ

N'importe qui peut être grand, parce que n'importe qui peut être utile. Il n'est pas obligatoire d'avoir un diplôme universitaire pour être utile. Il n'est pas nécessaire de pouvoir accorder le verbe avec le sujet pour être utile. Il n'est pas nécessaire de connaître Platon et Aristote pour être utile. Il n'est pas nécessaire de connaître la théorie de la relativité de Einstein pour être utile. Il n'est pas nécessaire de connaître la deuxième théorie de la thermodynamique pour être utile. On a seulement besoin d'un coeur plein de bonne volonté et d'une âme guidée par l'amour.

MARTIN LUTHER KING JR. (1929-1968)

American Civil Rights Leader
Líder Americano de los Derechos Civiles
Leader américain des Droits Civils

Iron rusts from disuse; stagnant water loses its purity and in cold weather becomes frozen even so does inaction sap the vigors of the mind.

৪০তেও

El hierro se enmohece si no se usa, el agua estancada pierde su pureza y se congela en tiempo frío; de igual modo la inacción debilita el vigor de la mente.

৪০তেও

Le fer se rouille si on ne l'utilise pas; l'eau stagnante perd sa pureté et se congèle en hiver; de la même manière, l'inaction sape la vigueur mentale.

LEONARDO DA VINCI (1452-1519)

Italian Painter, Sculptor, Architect, Engineer & Sage
Pintor, Escultor, Arquitecto, Ingeniero & Sabio Italiano
Peintre, sculpteur, architecte, ingénieur et savant italien

January 17
17 de enero
17 janvier

To be good is the natural tendency of mankind like water that flows downward.

౭౦౭౩

La tendencia natural del hombre es hacia la bondad como lo es la tendencia del agua a fluir hacia abajo.

౭౦౭౩

Etre bon est la tendance naturelle de l'homme comme celle de l'eau qui coule vers le bas.

MENG-TSE (¿372?-289 B. C.)

Chinese Philosopher
Filósofo Chino
Philosophe chinois

January 18
18 de enero
18 janvier

One ounce of application is worth more than a ton of abstraction.

❧❧

Una onza de dedicación vale más que una tonelada de abstracción.

❧❧

Un gramme de pratique vaut plus qu'une tonne de théories.

BOOKER T. WASHINGTON (1856-1915)

American Educator
Educador Americano
Éducateur américain

Any woman who aspires to behave like a man lacks any ambition for sure.

ഇറ്റ

Cualquier mujer que aspira a comportarse como un hombre, seguramente no tiene ninguna ambición.

ഇറ്റ

Une femme qui aspire à se comporter comme un homme n'a certainement aucune ambition.

DOROTHY PARKER (1893-1967)

American Writer
Escritora Americana
Écrivaine américaine

We all live under the same sky, but we don't all have the same horizon.

☙❧

Todos vivimos bajo el mismo cielo, pero no tenemos todos el mismo horizonte.

☙❧

Nous vivons tous sous le même ciel, mais nous n'avons pas tous le même horizon.

KONRAD ADENAUER (1876-1967)

German Politician
Político Alemán
Politicien allemand

January 21
21 de enero
21 janvier

The new frontier lies not beyond the planets but within each one of us.

⊰⊱

La nueva frontera no se encuentra más allá de los planetas, sino dentro de cada uno de nosotros.

⊰⊱

La nouvelle frontière n'est pas au-delà des planètes; elle se trouve en chacun de nous.

PIERRE ELLIOT TRUDEAU (1919-2000)

Former Canadian Prime Minister
Pasado Primer Ministro Canadiense
Ancien Premier Ministre du Canada

There are no secrets to SUCCESS: Don't waste time looking for them. SUCCESS is the result of perfection, hard work, learning from failure, loyalty to those for whom you work and persistence.

ಐಿೞ

No existen secretos para triunfar. No pierda su tiempo en su búsqueda. El éxito es el resultado de la búsqueda de la perfección, del trabajo duro, de las lecciones del fracaso, de la lealtad hacia las personas para quienes uno trabaja y la persistencia.

ಐಿೞ

Il n'y a pas de secrets pour réussir. Ne perdez pas votre temps à les chercher. La réussite est le résultat de la perfection, du travail acharné, des leçons tirées des échecs, de la loyauté envers ceux pour qui on travaille et de la persévérance.

COLIN POWELL (b. 1937)

American General & Secretary of State
General Americano & Secretario de Estado
Général américain et Secrétaire d'État

January 23
23 de enero
23 janvier

A teacher affects eternity; he can never tell where his influence stops.

ഇറ

Un maestro influencia la eternidad; él nunca puede decir en donde se detiene esta influencia.

ഇറ

Un enseignant influence l'éternité; il ne pourra jamais savoir où s'arrête son influence.

HENRY BROOKS ADAMS (1838-1918)

American Historian, Author of *The Education of Henry Adams*
Historiador Americano, Autor de *La Educación de Henry Adams*
Historien américain, auteur de *The Education of Henry Adams*

"Know yourself" is a good saying but not in all situations. Very often, it is better to know others.

❧☙

"Conócete a tí mismo" es un buen dicho, pero no en todas las situaciones. En muchas ocasiones, es mejor conocer a los demás.

❧☙

"Connais-toi toi – même" est une maxime valable, mais pas dans toutes les situations. Bien souvent, il est préférable de connaître les autres.

MENANDER (342-292 B.C.)

Greek Poet & Comedian
Poeta & Cómico Griego
Poète et comédien grec

A man's character is his fate.

୫୦୯୫

El carácter de una persona es su destino.

୫୦୯୫

La personnalité d'un individu détermine son destin.

HERACLITUS (540-480 B.C.)

Greek Philopher
Filósofo Griego
Philosophe grec

We are all rich; some people know it and profit from their riches; others ignore it and waste them.

ৰাজ

Todos somos ricos; algunos lo saben y aprovechan sus riquezas. Otros lo ignoran y las desperdician.

ৰাজ

Nous sommes tous riches; certains le savent et profitent de leurs richesses, d'autres l'ignorent et gaspillent leurs richesses.

EDOUARD F. LAFONTANT (b. 1932)

Master Motivator
Maestro Motivador
Maître motivateur

January 27
27 de enero
27 janvier

If you keep judging people, you won't have time to love them.

፡ፚ፧

Si usted se pone a juzgar a la gente, no tendrá tiempo para amarlos.

፡ፚ፧

Si vous vous mettez à juger les autres, vous n'aurez pas le temps de les aimer.

AGNES GONXHA BOJAXHIU (1910-1997)

Mother Theresa of Calcutta
Madre Teresa de Calcuta
Mère Térèse de Calcutta

A leader is rated as mediocre when his subordinates have to obey and acclaim him and as the worst when they despise him. He is rated as great when, as his work is done and his goals attained, his subordinates proclaim: WE DID IT!

৪০০৪

El líder es considerado mediocre cuando la gente tiene que obedecer y aclamarlo. Es peor cuando la gente lo desprecia. Pero la gente va a decir del gran líder que habla poco cuando su trabajo está hecho y sus metas logradas: ¡LO HEMOS HECHO NOSOTROS MISMOS!

৪০০৪

Un leader est qualifié de médiocre quand ses subordonnés sont contraints de lui obéir et de le flatter, et qualifié de pire quand ils le méprisent. Il est qualifié de grand leader quand, après avoir accompli ses devoirs et atteint ses buts, ses subordonnés proclament avec fierté: C'EST NOUS QUI AVONS ACCOMPLI CE TRAVAIL!

LAO-TZU (500 B. C.)

Chinese Philosopher
Filósofo Chino
Philosophe chinois

January 29
29 de enero
29 janvier

Youth is happy because it has the capacity to see BEAUTY. Anyone who keeps the ability to see BEAUTY never grows old.

୨୦୦୪

La juventud es feliz porque tiene la capacidad de ver la BELLEZA. Cualquier persona que conserve la habilidad de ver la BELLEZA, nunca envejece.

୨୦୦୪

La jeunesse est heureuse parce qu'elle a la faculté de voir la BEAUTÉ. Ceux qui conservent cette faculté ne vieillissent jamais.

FRANZ KAFKA (1883-1924)

Czech Writer
Escritor Checo
Écrivain tchèque

Of all the systems of morality, ancient or modern, which have come under my observation, none appears to me so pure as that of Jesus.

೪⦿ೞ

De todos los sistemas de moralidad, antiguos o modernos, que he tenido la oportunidad de examinar, ninguno me parece tan puro como el de Jesús.

೪⦿ೞ

De tous les systèmes de moralité, anciens ou modernes, que j'ai eu l'occasion d'étudier, aucun ne me paraît aussi pur que celui de Jésus.

THOMAS JEFFERSON (1743-1826)

Third President of the United States of America
Tercer Presidente de los Estados Unidos de América
Troisième Président des États-Unis d'Amérique

January 31
31 de enero
31 janvier

There are only two kinds of immoral conduct. The first is due to indifference, thoughtlessness, failure to reflect upon what is for the common good. The second type of immorality is represented by the "unpardonable sin" of which Jesus spoke—deliberate refusal, after reflection, to follow the light when seen.

ᏮᏯᏳ

Hay dos clases de comportamiento inmoral. La primera es debido a la indiferencia, el descuido y la falta de reflexionar en lo que atañe al bien común. La segunda tiene que ver con lo que Jesús cataloga como un "pecado imperdonable", - el negarse deliberadamente después de reflexionar - de seguir el camino de la luz cuando la ve.

ᏮᏯᏳ

Il n'existe que deux catégories de conduite immorale: la première c'est l'indifférence, l'irresponsabilité et la négligence de chercher ce qui est bien pour l'humanité tout entière. La seconde est ce que Jésus a appelé "le péché impardonnable" qui consiste à refuser délibérément de suivre la lumière quand on l'a vue.

ROBERT MILLIKAN (1868-1953)

American Physicist
Físico Americano
Physicien américain

FEBRUARY — FEBRERO — FEVRIER

1 . . . . .DESMOND TUTU
2 . . . . .CHINESE PROVERB
3 . . . . .RAMSEY CLARK

4 . . . . .HENRIETE PRESSBURG
5 . . . . .FRANçOIS MARIE AROUET —
                              dit VOLTAIRE
6 . . . . .PAUL J. MEYER

7 . . . . .KURT HAHN
8 . . . . .RALPH WALDO EMERSON
9 . . . . .CALLIMACHUS

10 . . . . .MENANDER
11 . . . . .SIMONE HUTTINOT LAFONTANT
12 . . . . .EDOUARD F. LAFONTANT

13 . . . . .ALBERT CAMUS
14 . . . . .MENG-TSE
15 . . . . .JOSE MARTÍ

16 . . . . .THE BIBLE
17 . . . . .JAMES ALLEN
18 . . . . .LUIS MUÑOZ MARÍN

19 . . . . .LUIS A. FERRÉ
20 . . . . .MARCUS AURELIUS ANTONINUS
21 . . . . .HENRY FORD

22 . . . . .MARIANNE WILLIAMSON
23 . . . . .PABLO CASALS
24 . . . . .RAY KROC

25 . . . . .OLIVER WENDELL HOLMES
26 . . . . .W. EDWARD DEMING
27 . . . . .AKOUSA BUSIA

28 . . . . .THOMAS JEFFERSON
29 . . . . .JORGE L. BORGES

We believe that we are in fact the image of our Creator. Our response must be to live up to that amazing potential—to give God glory by reflecting His beauty and His love. That is why we are here and that is the purpose of our lives. In that response we enter most fully into relationship with God, our fellow men and women, and we are in harmony with all creation.

৪০০৪

Creemos que de hecho somos la imagen de nuestro Creador. Nuestra respuesta debe ser de vivir según este desafío extraordinario, o sea, dar gloria a Dios reflejando Su belleza y Su amor. Es por eso que estamos en esta tierra y también es el propósito de nuestra vida. Así entramos en comunión con Dios y con los otros seres humanos en armonía con toda la creación.

৪০০৪

Nous croyons fermement que nous sommes l'image de notre Créateur. Nous devons donc vivre en fonction de ce défi extraordinaire et rendre gloire à Dieu en reflétant Sa beauté et Son amour. C'est pourquoi nous sommes sur cette terre et c'est le but de la vie. Ainsi, nous communions avec Dieu et le genre humain en harmonie avec toute la création.

DESMOND TUTU (b. 1931)

Anglican Archbishop of Capetown, South Africa
Arzobispo Anglicano de Capetown, Sur Africa
Archevêque anglican de Capetown, Afrique du Sud

Renew yourself completely, each day do it again, once again and always again.

&⚬⅏

Renuévese completamente, cada día hágalo de nuevo, otra vez de nuevo y siempre de nuevo.

&⚬⅏

Renouvelez-vous complètement, chaque jour faites-le de nouveau, encore une fois et toujours.

CHINESE PROVERB
PROVERBIO CHINO
PROVERBE CHINOIS

February 3
3 de febrero
3 février

Turbulence is life force. It is opportunity. Let's love turbulence and use it for change.

৪০০৪

Turbulencia es la fuerza de la vida. Ahí está nuestra oportunidad. Amemos la turbulencia y usémosla para hacer cambios.

৪০০৪

L'agitation est la force de la vie. C'est là que se trouve l'opportunité. Aimons donc l'agitation, et utilisons la pour changer les choses.

RAMSEY CLARK (b. 1927)

Former Attorney General of the United States of America
Ex Secretario del Depto. de Justicia de los Estados Unidos de América
Ex-secrétaire du Département de la Justice des Etats-Unis
d'Amérique

If Karl Marx, instead of writing about capital, had made a lot of capital, it would have been much better.

৪৩৫৪

Si Karl Marx, en vez de escribir sobre el capital, hubiera hecho mucho capital, sería mucho mejor.

৪৩৫৪

Si Karl Marx, au lieu d'écrire sur le capital, avait accumulé un capital, c'eût été bien mieux.

HENRIETTE PRESSBURG

Mother of Karl Marx
La madre de Karl Marx
La mère de Karl Marx

February 5
5 de febrero
5 février

I detest what you write, but I will give my life to defend your freedom to write.

୨୦୯୫

Detesto lo que usted escribe, pero daré mi vida para defender su derecho a seguir escribiendo.

୨୦୯୫

Je déteste ce que vous écrivez, mais je donnerai ma vie pour défendre votre liberté d'écrire.

FRANçOIS MARIE AROUET — dit VOLTAIRE (1694-1778)

French Writer
Escritor Francés
Écrivain français

February 6
6 de febrero
6 février

If you don't have discipline, you don't have anything. If you have discipline, EVERYTHING IS POSSIBLE.

ಬುಲ

Si usted no tiene disciplina, no tiene nada. Si usted tiene disciplina, TODO ES POSIBLE.

ಬುಲ

Si vous n'avez pas de discipline, vous n'avez rien. Si vous en avez, alors TOUT EST POSSIBLE.

PAUL J. MEYER (b. 1928)

American Entrepreneur & Educator
Founder of the Success Motivation Institute companies
Empresario & Educador Americano
Fundador de las Empresas Success Motivation Institute
Homme d'affaires et éducateur américain
Fondateur des entreprises Success Motivation Institute

February 7
7 de febrero
7 février

There is more in us than we know. If we can be made to see it, perhaps, for the rest of our life, we will be unwilling to settle for less.

ಶಿ೦೮೫

Sabemos muy poco de nosotros. Si hacemos el esfuerzo de conocernos más, quizás por el resto de nuestra vida, seremos más exigentes con nosotros.

ಶಿ೦೮೫

Nous savons très peu de nous-mêmes. Si nous faisons l'effort de mieux nous connaître, peut être nous deviendrons plus exigeants envers nous-mêmes le reste de notre vie.

KURT HAHN (1886-1974)

German Educator & Founder of Outward Bound
Educador Alemán & Fundador de Outward Bound
Éducateur allemand et fondateur de Outward Bound

Thoughts rule the world.

℘℘℘

Los pensamientos gobiernan el mundo.

℘℘℘

Les pensées mènent le monde.

RALPH WALDO EMERSON (1803-1882)

American Philosopher
Filósofo Americano
Philosophe américain

February 9
9 de febrero
9 février

A good man never dies.

ༀༀ

Un hombre de bien nunca muere.

ༀༀ

Un homme de bien ne meurt jamais.

CALLIMACHUS (c. 305-c. 240 B.C.)

Alexandrian Poet
Poeta Alejandrino
Poète alexandrin

Art is a man's refuge from adversity.

೮೦೦೮

El arte es donde se refugia el hombre en la adversidad.

೮೦೦೮

Dans l'adversité, l'art est le refuge de l'homme.

MENANDER (342-292 B.C.)

Greek Poet & Comedian
Poeta & Cómico Griego
Poète et comédien grec

February 11
11 de febrero
11 février

Pay more attention to the most humble; they will pay you back with a lot of gratitude—sometimes it's the only thing they have.

৪৩০৪

Dale más atención a los más humildes; te pagarán con mucha gratitud, lo único que, a veces, tienen para dar.

৪৩০৪

Accorde plus d'attention aux plus humbles; ils te seront très reconnaissants - parfois la gratitude est tout ce qu'ils ont à donner.

SIMONE HUTTINOT LAFONTANT (1909-1958)

A Haitian mother, my mother
Una madre haitiana, mi madre
Une mère haïtienne, ma mère

He failed in business in 1831 — he was twenty-two years old — and again in 1833. In 1832, he was defeated in a race for the Legislature. He was defeated for Congress in 1843 and elected in 1846 but defeated again in 1848. He was defeated in the Senate's election in 1855, for vice president in 1856 and again for the Senate in 1858. But, in 1860 he was elected president of the United States — at the age of fifty-one years old. Eight hundred fifty-six historians have chosen him as the best president yet. His name: ABRAHAM LINCOLN.

৪০০৪

Fracasó en los negocios en el 1831 - tenía 22 años - y de nuevo en el 1833. En el 1832 fue derrotado en unas elecciones legislativas. Fracasó otra vez en el 1843 en el Congreso pero fue elegido en el 1846 para perder otra vez en el 1848. Fue derrotado en las Elecciones Senatoriales del 1855, también en el 1856 para la Vicepresidencia y otra vez para el Senado en el 1858. Pero en el 1860, fue electo Presidente de los Estados Unidos de América - tenía 51 años. Ochocientos cincuenta y seis historiadores lo escogieron como el mejor Presidente de la Nación Americana. Su nombre: ABRAHAM LINCOLN.

৪০০৪

Il a échoué dans les affaires en 1831 - il avait 22 ans - et de nouveau en 1833. En 1832, il a subi une défaite aux élections législatives, il a encore échoué en 1843; enfin il fut élu en 1846 pour de nouveau perdre en 1848. Encore d'autres échecs: en 1855 dans les élections sénatoriales, en 1856 à la Vice-présidence et en 1858 au Sénat. Cependant, il fut élu en 1860 Président des États-Unis d'Amérique - il avait 51 ans. 856 historiens le considèrent comme le meilleur Président des États-Unis. Son nom: ABRAHAM LINCOLN.

EDOUARD F. LAFONTANT (b. 1932)

Master Motivator
Maestro Motivador
Maître motivateur

February 13
13 de febrero
13 février

Don't wait for the last judgement; it takes place every day.

&ດິຕຈ

No esperes por el juicio final; sucede cada día.

&ດິຕຈ

N'attends pas le jugement final; il arrive tous les jours.

ALBERT CAMUS (1913-1960)

French Writer
Escritor Francés
Écrivain français

The great man is he who does not lose his childhood heart.

ଚ୬ଓଃ

Un gran hombre es el que no ha perdido su corazón de niño.

ଚ୬ଓଃ

Un grand homme est celui qui n'a pas perdu son coeur d'enfant.

MENG-TSE (372-289 B.C.)

Chinese Philosopher
Filósofo Chino
Philosophe chinois

February 15
15 de febrero
15 février

Habits create an appeareance of justice; progress has no greater enemy than habits.

৪৩৫৪

Los hábitos crean la apariencia de justicia; el progreso no tiene un enemigo mayor que los hábitos.

৪৩৫৪

La routine crée une justice superficielle; le progrès n'a pas un ennemi plus grand que la routine.

JOSE MARTÍ (1853-1895)

Cuban Writer & Patriot
Escritor y Patriota Cubano
Écrivain et patriote cubain

I am the way, the truth and life.
Nobody can reach the Father but through me.
If you know me, you will also know my Father.
Now you know him and you saw him.

୫୬୯୧

Yo soy el camino, la verdad y la vida.
Nadie va al Padre, sino por mí.
Si me conocen a mí, también conocerán al Padre.
Desde ya ustedes lo conocen y lo han visto.

୫୬୯୧

Je suis la voie, la vérité et la vie.
Personne ne va au Père sans passer par moi.
Si tu me connais, tu connaîtras aussi mon Père.
Maintenant tu le connais et tu l'as vu.

THE BIBLE – LA BIBLIA – LA BIBLE

St. John 14:5-7
San Juan 14:5-7
Saint Jean 14:5-7

February 17
17 de febrero
17 février

Circumstance does not make the man; it reveals him to himself.

&OC3

Las circunstancias no hacen el hombre; ellas lo ayudan a conocerse.

&OC3

Les circonstances ne façonnent pas l'homme; elles le révèlent à lui-même.

JAMES ALLEN (1864-1912)

English Writer, Author of the book *As a Man Thinketh*
Escritor Inglés, Autor del libro *As a Man Thinketh*
Écrivain anglais, auteur du livre *As a Man Thinketh*

Education is the shifting of knowledge and responsibility from one generation to the next.

๛๏๛

La educación es la transferencia del conocimiento y de la responsabilidad de unas generaciones a otras.

๛๏๛

L'éducation est le transfert des connaissances et des responsabilités d'une génération à l'autre.

LUIS MUÑOZ MARÍN (1898-1980)

Former Governor of Puerto Rico
Ex Gobernador de Puerto Rico
Ex-gouverneur de Porto Rico

February 19
19 de febrero
19 février

Being young, it is not about age. It is keeping alive in the soul the illusions and the capacity to dream. It is living intensely with the heart full of self-confidence.

ﮗﮢﮬﮯ

Ser joven, no es tener pocos años. Es conservar viva la ilusión en el alma y despierta la capacidad en el espíritu para soñar; es vivir con intensidad y el corazón lleno de fe.

ﮗﮢﮬﮯ

Etre jeune n'est pas une question d'âge. Etre jeune, c'est conserver vivante l'illusion dans l'âme et maintenir éveillée dans l'esprit la capacité de rêver. Etre jeune c'est vivre intensément avec le coeur plein de confiance en soi.

LUIS A. FERRÉ (1904-2003)

Former Governor of Puerto Rico
Ex Gobernador de Puerto Rico
Ex-gouverneur de Porto Rico

February 20
20 de febrero
20 février

Look into yourself; there lies dormant a source of strength which will always spring up if you look.

&OCß

Mira dentro de tí; de allí siempre brota una fuente de fortaleza en cada mirada.

&OCß

Regardez en vous-même; là dort une source d'énergie qui jaillira toujours si vous regardez.

MARCUS AURELIUS ANTONINUS (121-180)

Roman Emperor & Philosopher
Emperador Romano & Filósofo
Empereur romain et philosophe

February 21
21 de febrero
21 février

Coming together is a beginning; keeping together is progress; working together is SUCCESS.

೮ುಚಿ

Empezar juntos es un comienzo; permanecer juntos es progreso; trabajar unidos es EXITO.

೮ುಚಿ

Entreprendre un projet ensemble est un début; rester ensemble c'est le progrès; travailler ensemble c'est la réussite.

HENRY FORD (1863-1947)

American Industrialist, Founder of the Ford Motor Company
Industrial Americano, Fundador de la Ford Motor Company
Industriel américain, fondateur de la Ford Motor Company

In every community, there is work to be done. In every nation, there are wounds to heal. In every heart, there is the power to do it.

ಬಂಛ

En cada comunidad hay trabajo que hacer; en cada país hay heridas que curar. En cada corazón, está el poder para hacerlo.

ಬಂಛ

Dans chaque communauté il y a du travail à réaliser; dans chaque pays il y a des blessures à cicatriser. Dans chaque coeur, il y a la force pour le faire.

MARIANNE WILLIAMSON

American Writer, Author of *Return to Love*
Escritora Americana, Autora de *Return to Love*
Écrivaine américaine, auteure de *Return to Love*

February 23
23 de febrero
23 février

We ought to understand that we are one of the leaves of a tree, and the tree is all humanity. We cannot live without the others, we cannot live without the tree.

ಬಂಬ

Debemos pensar que somos las hojas de un árbol y el árbol es toda la humanidad. No podemos vivir sin los demás, no podemos vivir sin el árbol.

ಬಂಬ

Nous devons comprendre que nous sommes tous les feuilles d'un même arbre et que cet arbre est l'humanité tout entière. Nous ne pouvons pas vivre sans les autres, nous ne pouvons pas vivre sans cet arbre.

PABLO CASALS (1878-1973)

Spanish Musician & Composer
Músico & Compositor Español
Musicien et compositeur espagnol

February 24
24 de febrero
24 février

I define salesmanship as the gentle art of letting your customers have what you want for them.

Defino la venta como el suave arte de dejar que los clientes tengan lo que queremos para ellos.

Je définis la profession de vendeur comme l'art subtil de vendre aux clients ce que vous avez choisi pour eux.

RAY KROC (1902-1984)

American Entrepreneur, Founder of McDonald's Restaurants
Hombre de Negocios Americano
Fundador de los Restaurantes McDonald
Homme d'Affaires Américain
Fondateur des restaurants McDonald

February 25
25 de febrero
25 février

Man's mind, stretched to a new idea, never goes back to its original dimensions.

୫୦୯୫

Cuando el espíritu de un hombre se estira con una nueva idea, nunca regresa a su dimensión original.

୫୦୯୫

Quand l'esprit d'un homme s'ouvre à une nouvelle idée, il ne revient jamais à sa dimension initiale.

OLIVER WENDELL HOLMES (1809-1894)

American Poet, Novelist & Physician
Poeta, Novelista & Médico Americano
Poète, romancier et médecin américain

Nothing happens without personal transformation.

ஐைௌ

Nada sucede sin transformación personal.

ஐைௌ

Rien ne se réalise sans une transformation personnelle.

W. EDWARD DEMING (1900-1994)

American Statitician & Educator
Father of the Third Industrial Revolution
Estadístico & Educador Americano
Padre de la Tercera Revolución Industrial
Statisticien et éducateur américain
Père de la Troisième Révolution industrielle

February 27
27 de febrero
27 février

Faith is not a leap into the darkness, but a stroll through light.

৪০৫৪

La fe no es un salto en la obscuridad, sino un paseo por la luz.

৪০৫৪

La foi n'est pas un saut dans l'obscurité, c'est plutôt une promenade à travers la lumière.

AKOUSA BUSIA

African Actress & Dramatist
Actriz & Dramaturga Africana
Actrice et dramaturge africaine

Eternal vigilance is the price of freedom.

&⊃⊂&

El precio de la libertad es la vigilancia eterna.

&⊃⊂&

La vigilance éternelle est le prix de la liberté.

THOMAS JEFFERSON (1743-1826)

3rd President of the United States of America
Tercer Presidente de los Estados Unidos de América
Troisième Président des États-Unis d'Amérique

February 29
29 de febrero
29 février

As the years go by, I have observed that beauty, like happiness is frequent. Not one day goes by without me feeling in paradise even for a moment.

                           ൟരঃ

Al cabo de los años he observado que la belleza, como la felicidad, es frecuente. No pasa un día en que estemos un instante en el paraíso.

                           ൟരঃ

Au fil des ans, j'ai remarqué que la beauté comme le bonheur n'était pas si rare. Il ne se passe pas un jour sans que j'aie l'impression d'être au paradis ne serait-ce que pour un moment.

JORGE LUIS BORGES (1899-1986)

Argentinian Writer & Poet
Escritor & Poeta Argentino
Écrivain et poète argentin

MARCH – MARZO – MARS

1 . . . . .HORACE MANN
2 . . . . .ST. ÉVREMOND
3 . . . . .RALPH WALDO EMERSON

4 . . . . .LUIGI PIRANDELO
5 . . . . .ELIE METCHNIKOFF
6 . . . . .IMMANUEL KANT

7 . . . . .HERACLITUS
8 . . . . .HELEN ADAMS KELLER
9 . . . . .SOR ISOLINA FERRÉ

10 . . . . .JOHN F. KENNEDY
11 . . . . .EDOUARD F. LAFONTANT
12 . . . . .THE BIBLE

13 . . . . .PAUL J. MEYER
14 . . . . .HENRY FORD
15 . . . . .CARL GUSTAV JUNG

16 . . . . .JOHANN WOLFGANG GOETHE
17 . . . . .JOSE MARTÍ
18 . . . . .BAIRD T. SPALDING III

19 . . . . .VIRGILE
20 . . . . .ALBERT CAMUS
21 . . . . .MORTIMER J. ADLER

22 . . . . .BLAISE PASCAL
23 . . . . .ANONYMOUS
24 . . . . .ELEANOR ROOSEVELT

25 . . . . .ANONYMOUS
26 . . . . .ANONYMOUS
27 . . . . .ZIG ZIGLAR

28 . . . . .VERNON E. JORDAN
29 . . . . .Hô-CHI MINH
30 . . . . .DRAYTON MCLANE

31 . . . . .JAMES ALLEN

Education . . . beyond all other devices of human origin is the great equalizer of conditions of man — the balance wheel of the social machinery.

৪৩৫৪

La educación, más allá de todas las invenciones de origen humano, es el gran nivelador de la condición humana - la rueda que equilibra la maquinaria social.

৪৩৫৪

L'éducation, de loin le meilleur outil inventé par l'homme, est la plus grande niveleuse de la societé humaine; c'est la pièce qui maintient l'équilibre de la machine sociale.

HORACE MANN (1796-1859)

American Educator
Educador Americano
Éducateur américain

Health is like wealth: it withdraws its favors from those who abuse it.

৪৩৫৪৩

La salud es como la fortuna: retira sus favores a los que abusan de ella.

৪৩৫৪৩

La santé est comme la fortune, elle retire ses faveurs à ceux qui en abusent.

SAINT-ÉVREMOND (1614-1703)

Charles de Marguetel
French Writer
Escritor Francés
Écrivain français

March 3
3 de marzo
3 mars

What your mind can conceive and believe, you can achieve.

&OCS

Usted puede realizar todo lo que su mente puede concebir y creer.

&OCS

Vous avez le pouvoir de réaliser tout ce que votre esprit peut concevoir et croire.

RALPH WALDO EMERSON (1803-1882)

American Philosopher, Poet & Essayist
Filósofo, Poeta & Ensayista Americano
Philosophe, poète et essayiste américain

March 4
4 de marzo
4 mars

All those who are already gone are still living in us.

∞

En nosotros siguen viviendo todos aquellos que se han marchado.

∞

En nous continuent à vivre tous ceux qui sont déjà partis.

LUIGI PIRANDELO (1867-1936)

Italian Writer
Escritor Italiano
Écrivain italien

A man is as old as his arteries.

୫୦ଓଃ

El hombre es tan viejo como sus arterias.

୫୦ଓଃ

L'homme a l'âge de ses artères.

ELIE METCHNIKOFF (1845-1916)

Russian-French Scientist
Científico Ruso-Francés
Scientifique franco-russe

All the gifts of nature, such as courage, resolution and perseverance may be in the highest degree pernicious and hurtful if the will which directs them, or what is called the "character," is not itself good.

∞☾∞

Todos los dones de la naturaleza como valentía, resolución y perseverancia pueden ser perniciosos y nocivos al más alto nivel si la voluntad que los anima o lo que llamamos "carácter" no es buena en sí.

∞☾∞

Tous les dons de la nature, tels que le courage, la volonté et la persévérance peuvent être nuisibles et dangereux au plus haut degré si la volonté qui les guide - ou ce que nous appelons la personnalité - n'est pas elle-même solide et bien équilibrée.

IMMANUEL KANT (1724-1804)

German Philosopher
Filósofo Alemán
Philosophe allemand

March 7
7 de marzo
7 mars

All is flux; nothing is stationary. There is nothing permanent except change.

ഌൽ

Todo fluye, nada es estable. No hay nada permanente excepto el cambio.

ഌൽ

Tout est mouvement, rien n'est inerte. La seule chose permanente c'est le changement.

HERACLITUS (540-480 B.C.)

Greek Philosopher
Filósofo Griego
Philosophe grec

Security is mostly a superstition. It does not exist in nature . . . Life is either a daring adventure or nothing.

ഇൗരു

La seguridad es generalmente un mito. No existe en la naturaleza . . . La vida es una atrevida aventura o nada.

ഇൗരു

La sécurité est plutôt un mythe. Elle n'existe pas dans la nature . . . La vie doit être une aventure pleine de défis, autrement elle est vide.

HELEN ADAMS KELLER (1880-1968)

Blind and deaf Author, Speaker & Philanthropist
Autora ciega y muda, oradora & filántropa
Auteure sourde-muette, oratrice et philanthrope

March 9
9 de marzo
9 mars

We cannot change the world, but we are going to change a small piece of the world around us.

ဆဝ၆ဒ

No podemos cambiar el mundo, pero vamos a cambiar un poquito del mundo que nos toca alrededor.

ဆဝ၆ဒ

Nous ne pouvons pas changer le monde, mais nous allons changer un petit morceau du monde qui nous entoure.

SOR ISOLINA FERRÉ (1914-2000)

Puerto Rican Catholic Nun
Monja Católica Puertorriqueña
Religieuse catholique portorricaine

March 10
10 de marzo
10 mars

Ask not what your country can do for you; ask what you can do for your country.

ಬಣಿ

No pregunte lo que su país puede hacer por usted; pregunte lo que usted puede hacer por su país.

ಬಣಿ

Ne demandez pas ce que votre pays peut faire pour vous, demandez plutôt ce que vous pouvez faire pour votre pays.

JOHN F. KENNEDY (1917-1963)

35th President of the United States of America
35° Presidente de los Estados Unidos
35e Président des États-Unis d'Amérique

March 11
11 *de marzo*
11 *mars*

Your attitude is not like your fingerprints or the composition of your DNA*; you can choose it, and you can change it. The choice is yours.

ಸಿಂಡ

La actitud no es como sus huellas digitales o la composición de su ADN**; puede cambiarla. La elección es suya.

ಸಿಂಡ

Contrairement à vos empreintes digitales ou à la composition de votre ADN***, votre attitude est quelque chose que vous pouvez choisir ou changer. Ce choix vous appartient.

EDOUARD F. LAFONTANT (b. 1932)

Master Motivator
Maestro Motivador
Maître motivateur

*Deoxyribonucleic acid
**Acido Desoxirribo nucleico
*** Acide désoxyribonucléique

Trust in the Lord with all your heart, and lean not on your own understanding; in all your ways acknowledge Him, and He shall direct your paths.

ഇൗ

Confía en Yavé sin reserva alguna, no te apoyes en tu inteligencia. En todas tus empresas ténle presente, y el dirigirá todos tus pasos.

ഇൗ

Aie confiance en Yahweh de tout ton coeur, et ne compte pas seulement sur ta propre intelligence. Dans toutes tes décisions, pense à Lui et Il les rendra moins difficiles.

THE BIBLE — LA BIBLIA — LA BIBLE

Proverbs 3:5-6
Proverbios 3:5-6
Proverbes 3:5-6

You can have anything you want in life if you crystallize your thinking. You alone control your destiny.

୨୦ଓଔ

Usted puede tener todo lo que quiera en la vida si usted cristaliza su pensamiento. Sólo usted controla su destino.

୨୦ଓଔ

Vous pouvez avoir tout ce que vous désirez dans la vie si vous cristallisez vos pensées. Vous seul contrôlez votre destin.

PAUL J. MEYER (b. 1928)

American Entrepreneur & Educator
Founder of the Success Motivation Institute Companies
Empresario & Educador Americano
Fundador de las Empresas Success Motivation Institute
Homme d'affaires et éducateur américain
Fondateur des entreprises Success Motivation Institute

Many so-called "economic" problems are only the ignorance of the directors of business. The business itself does not fail, but the man who is the "boss" of a business that does not know to its last operative detail is certain of failure before he begins. Whatever your goal in life, the beginning is knowledge and experience— or, briefly, work.

৪০৫৪

Muchos de los problemas llamados 'económicos' son solamente la ignorancia de los directores de negocios. El negocio en sí no fracasa; la persona que es el 'jefe' de un negocio que no conoce hasta el último detalle operacional de su negocio es un seguro fracaso antes de empezar. No importa cuál es su meta en la vida, el principio es conocimiento y experiencia - o simplemente trabajo.

৪০৫৪

Beaucoup de problèmes soi-disant économiques sont en réalité imputables à l'ignorance de certains directeurs d'entreprise. Une entreprise n'échoue pas toute seule, cependant si le directeur ne connaît pas son entreprise dans ses moindres détails, il échouera certainement avant même de commencer. Quel que soit votre but dans la vie, le début exige le savoir et l'expérience, autrement dit le travail.

HENRY FORD (1863-1947)

American Industrialist, Founder of the Ford Motor Company
Industrial Americano, Fundador de la Ford Motor Company
Industriel américain, fondateur de la Ford Motor Company

March 15
15 de marzo
15 mars

As far as we can discern, the sole purpose of human existence is to kindle a light in the darkness of mere being.

℞℟

Según lo que puedo comprender, el único propósito de la existencia humana es de prender una luz en la obscuridad de la simple existencia.

℞℟

A mon entendement, l'unique but de l'existence humaine est d'apporter un peu de clarté aux ténèbres du pourquoi de l'existence même.

CARL GUSTAV JUNG (1875-1961)

Swiss Psychologist
Psicólogo Suizo
Psychologue suisse

Treat a man like he is and he will stay what he is. Treat a man like he can and should be and he will become what he can and should be.

&OCG

Trata a un hombre tal como es y seguirá siendo lo que es. Trata a un hombre como puede y debe ser y se convertirá en lo que puede y debe ser.

&OCG

Traitez un homme comme il est et il restera ce qu'il est. Traitez un homme comme il peut et devrait être et il deviendra ce qu'il peut et devrait être.

JOHANN WOLFGANG GOETHE (1749-1832)

German Poet & Writer
Poeta & Escritor Alemán
Poète et écrivain allemand

March 17
17 de marzo
17 mars

A true man does not look where he will live better but where the duty is.

&0C3

El verdadero hombre no mira de qué lado se vive mejor sino, de qué lado está el deber.

&0C3

L'homme véritable ne cherche pas l'endroit où il vivra mieux mais ira là où le devoir l'appelle.

JOSE MARTÍ (1853-1895)

Cuban Writer & Patriot
Escritor & Patriota Cubano
Écrivain et patriote cubain

Man can choose to ascend toward the celestial heights that will elevate him beyond the mist of doubt, fear, sin and diseases or to fall into the filthy depth of human animality.

⚜

El hombre puede escoger ascender a las alturas celestiales que lo elevarán más allá de la bruma de la duda, del miedo, del pecado y de las enfermedades o caer en las profundidades sórdidas de la animalidad humana.

⚜

L'homme peut opter pour l'ascension vers les hauteurs célestes qui l'élèveront au-dessus des brouillards du doute, de la peur, du péché, et de la maladie, ou pour la chute vers les profondeurs sordides de l'animalité humaine.

BAIRD T. SPALDING III (1857-1953)

British Engineer & Writer
Author of *The Life & Teaching of the Masters of the Far East*
Ingeniero & Escritor Británico
Autor de *The Life & Teaching of the Masters of the Far East*
Ingénieur et écrivain britannique
Auteur de *The Life & Teaching of the Masters of the Far East*

It is the spirit that moves matter.

ಶಿಂಡ

El espíritu anima la masa.

ಶಿಂಡ

C'est l'esprit qui anime la matière.

VIRGILE (70–10 B.C.)

Latin Poet
Poeta Latino
Poète latin

Beauty is unbearable . . . offering us for a minute a glimpse into eternity that we would like to keep forever.

෨෦෬

La belleza es insoportable, ofreciéndonos por un minuto una mirada hacia la eternidad que quisiéramos extender para siempre.

෨෦෬

La beauté est insupportable, nous offrant pour une minute un regard sur l'éternité que nous aimerions conserver pour toujours.

ALBERT CAMUS (1913-1960)

French Writer
Escritor Francés
Écrivain français

Human resources are the nation's greatest potential riches; to squander them is to impoverish our future.

ೲೞ

Los recursos humanos son la mayor riqueza de la nación. Malgastarlos es empobrecer nuestro futuro.

ೲೞ

Les ressources humaines constituent la plus grande richesse de la nation. Gaspiller cette richesse, c'est ruiner notre avenir.

MORTIMER J. ADLER (1902-2001)

American Educator
Author of *The Paideia Proposal*
Educador Americano
Autor de *The Paideia Proposal*
Éducateur américain
Auteur de *The Paideia Proposal*

To see a person's qualities, it is not necessary to observe his outstanding accomplishments; just look at his daily routine.

৪০৫৪

Para mirar las virtudes de un hombre no hay que mirar sus esfuerzos extraordinarios, sino su vida cotidiana.

৪০৫৪

Il n'est pas nécessaire pour connaître les vertus d'une personne d'observer ses actions exceptionnelles; sa vie quotidienne suffit.

BLAISE PASCAL (1623-1662)

French Mathmatician, Phycisist, Philosopher & Writer
Matemático, Físico, Filósofo & Escritor Francés
Mathématicien, physicien, philosophe et écrivain français

March 23
23 de marzo
23 mars

We are all on planet Earth for a limited time. The purpose of our stay is to develop the potential God put in us, so that we can contribute more than we have received and make sure we did not live in vain.

80CB

Todos somos pasajeros sobre el planeta tierra; el propósito de nuestro viaje es desarrollar el potencial que Dios ha puesto en nosotros, de manera que podamos contribuir más de lo que hemos recibido y asegurarnos de no haber vivido en vano.

80CB

Nous sommes tous de passage sur la planète Terre; le but de notre séjour est de développer les dons reçus de Dieu de façon à pouvoir contribuer plus que ce que nous avons reçu et ainsi donner un sens à notre vie.

ANONYMOUS
ANONIMO
ANONYM

Nobody can make you feel inferior without your consent.

৪৩৫৪

Nadie puede hacerte sentir inferior sin tu consentimiento.

৪৩৫৪

Personne ne peut vous donner le sentiment d'être inférieur sans votre consentement.

ELEANOR ROOSEVELT (1884-1962)

Diplomat, Humanitarian
Wife of 32nd President of the United States of America
Diplomática, Humanista
Esposa del 32° Presidente de los Estados Unidos de América
Diplomate, Humaniste
Epouse du 32e Président des Etats Unis d'Amérique

March 25
25 de marzo
25 mars

The ships are safe in their harbors, but they were not built for that.

೪ುಲ

Los barcos están seguros en los puertos, pero no fueron construidos para eso.

೪ುಲ

Les navires sont en sécurité dans leur port, mais ils n'ont pas été construits pour y rester.

ANONYMOUS
ANONIMO
ANONYME

The only person who can stop you from becoming what God intends you to become is you.

ॐ

La única persona que puede impedir que usted se convierta en lo que Dios quiere para usted es usted mismo.

ॐ

Vous êtes la seule personne capable de vous empêcher de devenir ce que Dieu veut que vous soyez.

ANONYMOUS
ANONIMO
ANONYME

March 27
27 de marzo
27 mars

People often say that motivation doesn't last. Well, neither does bathing—that's why we recommend it daily.

ఌఓ

La gente dice que la motivación no dura. ¡Bueno! Su baño cotidiano tampoco. Es por eso que se lo recomendamos todos los días.

ఌఓ

On dit que la motivation ne dure pas, mais le bain non plus! C'est pourquoi nous recommandons une dose journalière de motivation.

ZIG ZIGLAR

American Motivator
Motivador Americano
Motivateur américain

We exist temporarily through what we take, but we live forever through what we give.

ജ്യോ

Vivimos temporalmente de lo que recibimos, pero vivimos por siempre de lo que damos.

ജ്യോ

Ce que nous recevons nous aide à subsister un certain temps, mais ce que nous donnons nous aide à vivre pour toujours.

VERNON E. JORDAN

American Civic Leader
Líder Cívico Americano
Leader civique américain

March 29
29 de marzo
29 mars

The darker the night, the nearer the sunrise.

ରେ୯ଓ

Más negra la noche, más cerca el amanecer.

ରେ୯ଓ

Plus noire la nuit, plus proche l'aube.

Hô-CHI MINH (1890-1969)

Vietnamese Patriot
Patriota Vietnamita
Patriote vietnamien

Leadership is a timeless river flowing endlessly toward the great vast tomorrow. Equally timeless is the need to shape and mold the river's channels. The unceasing effort to remanufacture leadership continues as men and women seek new ways to guide, manage and motivate others.

ঔৈৎ৪

El liderato es un eterno río que fluye sin cesar hacia el inmenso mañana. Eterna también es la necesidad de formar y moldear los canales del río. El esfuerzo de continuar el reinventar el liderato sigue mientras buscamos nuevas maneras de guiar, de facilitar y de motivar a nuestra gente.

ঔৈৎ৪

Le leadership est un fleuve sans fin qui coule sans cesse vers l'immensité du futur. Sans fin aussi est le besoin de modifier et d'orienter le cours de ce fleuve. L'effort permanent et continu pour remodeler le leadership demeure vivant grâce aux hommes et aux femmes qui cherchent de nouvelles méthodes pour guider, diriger et motiver les autres.

DRAYTON MCLANE

American Business Leader
From the Foreword of *Bridging the Leadership Gap*
by Paul J. Meyer & Randy Slechta
Hombre de Negocios Americano
Del Prefacio del libro *Bridging the Leadership Gap*
por Paul J. Meyer & Randy Slechta
Homme d'affaires américain
Préface du livre *Bridging the Leadership Gap*
Par Paul J. Meyer & Randy Slechta

March 31
31 de marzo
31 mars

A strong man cannot help a weaker man unless that weaker man is willing to be helped, and even then the weak man must become strong by himself; he must, by his own efforts, develop the strength which he admires in another. None but himself can alter his condition.

☙❧

Un hombre fuerte no puede ayudar a uno más débil a menos que el débil esté dispuesto a dejarse ayudar y aún entonces este hombre débil debería tratar de ser fuerte, de adquirir por sus propios esfuerzos la fortaleza que admira en el otro. Pues sólo el puede alterar su condición.

☙❧

Un homme fort ne peut pas aider un plus faible sans l'accord de ce dernier. Même dans ce cas, le faible devra devenir fort par ses propres efforts en développant la force qu'il admire dans l'autre. Personne d'autre que lui ne peut modifier son état.

JAMES ALLEN (1864-1912)

English Writer, Author of the book *As a Man Thinketh*
Escritor Inglés, Autor de libro *As a Man Thinketh*
Écrivain anglais, auteur du livre *As a Man Thinketh*

APRIL – ABRIL – AVRIL

1 . . . . .WILLIAM SOMERSET MAUGHAM
2 . . . . .RUSSIAN PROVERB
3 . . . . .HENRY DAVID THOREAU

4 . . . . .WERNHER VON BRAUN
5 . . . . .PAUL J. MEYER
6 . . . . .ANDRÉ MALRAUX

7 . . . . .CHINESE PROVERB
8 . . . . .MARY ALELON
9 . . . . .ANONYMOUS

10 . . . . .INDIRA GANDHI
11 . . . . .LA ROCHEFOUCAULD
12 . . . . .WILLIAM BLAKE

13 . . . . .JOHANN WOLFGANG GOETHE
14 . . . . .DONALD A. ADAMS
15 . . . . .ANONYMOUS

16 . . . . .ANONYMOUS
17 . . . . .THOMAS J. WATSON JR.
18 . . . . .AUGUSTE RODIN

19 . . . . .STEUART HENDERSON BRIT
20 . . . . .MARCO TULIO CICERON
21 . . . . .HENRI BERGSON

22 . . . . .EDOUARD F. LAFONTANT
23 . . . . .ABRAHAM LINCOLN
24 . . . . .SAM M. WALTON

25 . . . . .JAMES ALLEN
26 . . . . .FRIEDRICH HEGEL
27 . . . . .ANONYMOUS

28 . . . . .DICK GREGORY
29 . . . . .EUGENIO MARÍA DE HOSTOS
30 . . . . .MORTIMER J. ADLER

April 1
1 de abril
1er avril

April Fools' is a day to remind us what we are the rest of the year.

୫୬ର୍ଷ

El 1ro. de abril * - el día de los "inocentes" o de los "tontos" - es un día para recordarnos lo que somos los otros días del año.

୫୬ର୍ଷ

Poisson d'avril** - Le 1er. avril - est un jour qui nous rappelle ce que nous sommes les autres jours de l'année.

* En la cultura hispánica se celebra el 28 de diciembre, día de los Santos Inocentes.

** In France the fooled person is called "Poisson d'avril".

WILLIAM SOMERSET MAUGHAM (1874-1965)

British Writer
Escritor Británico
Écrivain britannique

April 2
2 de abril
2 avril

A man is good when he contributes to the betterment of others.

ಶ♥ಜ

Un hombre es bueno cuando hace mejores a los otros.

ಶ♥ಜ

Un homme est bon quand il contribue à rendre les autres meilleurs.

RUSSIAN PROVERB
PROVERBIO RUSO
PROBERBE RUSSE

April 3
3 de abril
3 avril

Changing the quality of every day of our lives: this is the highest of the arts.

ଞଔ

Cambiar la calidad de cada día de nuestras vidas; ésta es la más excelsa de las artes.

ଞଔ

Changer la qualité de chaque jour de notre vie, voilà le sommet de tous les arts.

HENRY DAVID THOREAU (1817-1862)

American Writer
Escritor Americano
Écrivain américain

I have learned to use the word "impossible" with the greatest care.

⊱✺⊰

He aprendido a utilizar la palabra "imposible" con muchísima cautela.

⊱✺⊰

J'ai appris à utiliser le mot "impossible" avec beaucoup de précaution.

WERNHER VON BRAUN (1912-1977)

German-American Physicist
Físico Germano-Americano
Physicien germano-américain

April 5
5 de abril
5 avril

Like an invisible magnet, positive attitudes reach out and draw into our presence the results that we so intensely wish to attract.

⚜

Como un imán invisible los pensamientos positivos alcanzan y atraen frente a nosotros los resultados que intensamente deseamos conseguir.

⚜

Comme un aimant invisible, les attitudes positives atteignent et attirent vers nous les résultats que nous désirons atteindre si intensément.

PAUL J. MEYER (b. 1928)

American Entrepreneur & Educator
Founder of The Success Motivation Institute's Companies
Empresario & Educador Americano
Fundador de las Empresas Success Motivation Institute
Homme d'affaires et éducateur américain
Fondateur des Entreprises Success Motivation Institute

We don't know how to resurrect bodies, but we have started to learn how to resurrect dreams.

❧❦

No sabemos resucitar los cuerpos, pero empezamos a saber cómo resucitar los sueños.

❧❦

Nous ne savons pas ressusciter les corps, mais nous commençons à savoir ressusciter les rêves.

ANDRÉ MALRAUX (1901-1976)

French Writer
Escritor Francés
Écrivain français

April 7
7 de abril
7 avril

If someone has difficulties in giving you a smile, give him one.

৪৩৬৪

Si alguien tiene dificultades para darte una sonrisa, dále la tuya.

৪৩৬৪

Si quelqu'un a des difficultés à vous gratifier d'un sourire, offrez-lui le vôtre.

CHINESE PROVERB
PROVERBIO CHINO
PROVERBE CHINOIS

Selling is the transference of feelings. We are in the business of making people feel good.

ಐಲ

El arte de vender es la transferencia de sentimientos. Estamos en el negocio de hacer que la gente se sienta bien.

ಐಲ

Vendre est l'art de provoquer des sensations; notre métier à nous, c'est de vendre du bien-être.

MARY ALELON

National Director, Mary Kay Cosmetics
Directora Nacional de Mary Kay Cosmetics
Directrice nationale de Mary Kay Cosmetics

April 9
9 de abril
9 avril

A politician thinks about the next election; a statesman thinks about the next generation.

֍

Un político piensa en las próximas elecciones; un hombre de estado en la próxima generación.

֍

Un politicien pense aux prochaines élections; un homme d'état pense à la prochaine génération.

ANONYMOUS
ANONIMO
ANONYME

There are two kinds of people: those who do the work and those who take the credit. Try to be in the first group. There is less competition there.

ಬಿಂದ

Hay dos clases de personas. Los que hacen el trabajo y los que se apoderan del reconocimiento por el trabajo de otros. Busca colocarte en el primer grupo, ahí hay menos competencia.

ಬಿಂದ

Il y a deux catégories d' individus: ceux qui font le travail et ceux qui en profitent. Cherchez à vous placer dans le premier groupe, où la compétition est moindre.

INDIRA GANDHI (1917-1984)

Former Prime Minister of India
Ex Primer Ministro de la India
Ex-Première Ministre de l'Inde

April 11
11 *de abril*
11 *avril*

A sure way to be fooled is to believe that you are smarter than the others.

৪৩৫

El camino recto para ser engañado es creerse más listo que los demás.

৪৩৫

La meilleure façon de se tromper est de se croire plus malin que les autres.

FRANçOIS DUC DE LA ROCHEFOUCAULD (1613-1680)
French Writer
Escritor Francés
Écrivain français

April 12
12 de abril
12 avril

I think people can be happy in this world and I know this world is one of imagination and vision.

৪৩৫৪৩

Creo que el hombre puede ser feliz en su propio mundo, y sé que este mundo es un producto de su imaginación y de su visión.

৪৩৫৪৩

Je pense que les gens peuvent être heureux en ce monde et je sais que ce monde est une oeuvre d'imagination et de vision.

WILLIAM BLAKE (1757-1827)

British Poet
Poeta Británico
Poète britannique

April 13
13 de abril
13 avril

The only ones who deserve freedom are those who know how to conquer it every day.

ଞଠଓଃ

Sólo merece libertad en la vida quien diariamente sabe conquistarla.

ଞଠଓଃ

Seuls méritent la liberté ceux qui savent la conquérir tous les jours.

JOHANN WOLFGANG GOETHE (1749-1832)

German Poet
Poeta Alemán
Poète allemand

To give real service, you must add something which cannot be bought or measured with money, and that is sincerity and integrity.

⊰⊱

Para dar un servicio de alta calidad, usted debe añadir algo que no se pueda comprar o medir con dinero; y eso es sinceridad e integridad.

⊰⊱

Pour offrir un service de haute qualité, vous devez y ajouter quelque chose que l'on ne peut pas acheter ou mesurer avec de l'argent: c'est la sincérité et l'intégrité.

DONALD A. ADAMS

President of Rotary International
Presidente de Rotary International
Président du Rotary International

April 15
15 de abril
15 avril

What you are is God's gift to you; what you become is your gift to God.

સ∾ભ્ર

Lo que tú eres es un regalo de Dios; lo que llegues a ser es tu regalo a Dios.

સ∾ભ્ર

Ce que tu es est un cadeau de Dieu; ce que tu deviens est ton cadeau à Dieu.

ANONYMOUS
ANONIMO
ANONYME

April 16
16 de abril
16 avril

Give the world the best that you have, and the best will come back to you.

 handy{CENTER}

ঔ৩৫ও

Dé al mundo lo mejor de usted y lo mejor regresará a usted.

ঔ৩৫ও

Donnez au monde le meilleur de vous-même et le meilleur vous reviendra.

ANONYMOUS
ANONIMO
ANONYME

April 17
17 de abril
17 avril

You have to put your heart in your business and your business in your heart.

❧❦

Usted tiene que poner su corazón en su negocio y su negocio en su corazón.

❧❦

Vous devez mettre votre coeur dans votre entreprise et votre entreprise dans votre coeur.

THOMAS J. WATSON JR. (1914-1993)

CEO International Business Machines (IBM)
P.D.G. International Business Machines (IBM)
P.D.G. International Business Machines (IBM)

April 18
18 de abril
18 avril

Where everyone thinks the same way, nobody is thinking.

ಬಂಗ

Donde todos piensan igual, nadie piensa.

ಬಂಗ

Là où tous pensent de la même manière, personne ne pense.

AUGUSTE RODIN (1840-1917)

French Sculptor (*The Thinker*)
Escultor Francés (*El Pensador*)
Sculpteur français (*Le Penseur*)

April 19
19 *de abril*
19 *avril*

Doing business without advertising is like winking at a girl in the dark. You know what you are doing, but nobody else does.

ɞɞCȜ

Hacer negocio sin publicidad es como guiñar a una mujer en la obscuridad. Usted sabe lo que está haciendo pero nadie más lo sabe.

ɞɞCȜ

Faire du commerce sans publicité, c'est comme faire de l'oeil à une femme dans l'obscurité. Vous savez ce que vous faites, mais personne d'autre ne le sait.

STEUART HENDERSON BRIT (b. 1907)

American Journalist – *NY Herald Tribune* 30-10-56
Periodista Americano – *NY Herald Tribune* 30-10-56
Journaliste américain – *NY Herald Tribune* 30-10-56

April 20
20 de abril
20 avril

As a field, however fertile, cannot be fruitful without cultivation, neither can a mind without learning.

෯ඏ

De la misma manera que un campo aunque sea fértil no puede ser productivo sin ser cultivado; una mente tampoco puede sin aprendizaje.

෯ඏ

De même qu'un champ, même fertile, ne peut être productif sans être cultivé, l'esprit ne peut rien produire sans les études.

MARCO TULIO CICERON (106-43 B.C.)

Roman Politician, Thinker & Public Speaker
Político, Pensador & Orador Romano
Homme politique, penseur et orateur romain

April 21
21 de abril
21 avril

To exist is to change; to change is to mature; to mature is to create oneself indefinitely.

8003

Existir es cambiar, cambiar es madurar, madurar es crearse uno a sí mismo indefinidamente.

8003

Exister c'est changer, changer c'est mûrir, mûrir c'est se créer soi-même indéfiniment.

HENRI BERGSON (1859-1941)

French Philosopher
Filósofo Francés
Philosophe français

Sir Isaac Newton said that if he has seen further than most men, it is by standing on the shoulders of giants; so I am convinced that by feeding your mind with positive thoughts daily, then yearly and forever, you too will become a giant.

ଝୠଔ

Sir Isaac Newton dijo que si él ha visto más allá que la mayoría de la gente, es porque él se puso encima de los hombros de los gigantes. Así llegué a la convicción que si usted repite estas ideas positivas todos los días, todos los años y siempre, usted también será un gigante.

ଝୠଔ

Sir Isaac Newton a dit qu' il voyait plus loin que la plupart des hommes en se tenant debout sur les épaules des géants. Partant de ce principe, je peux affirmer qu'en nourissant notre esprit d'idées positives, chaque jour, chaque année et toujours, nous aussi deviendrons des géants.

EDOUARD F. LAFONTANT (b. 1932)

Master Motivator
Maestro Motivador
Master motivateur

April 23
23 de abril
23 avril

Most folks are about as happy as they make up their minds to be.

৪৩৫৪

La mayoría de la gente son tan felices como decidan serlo.

৪৩৫৪

On devient aussi heureux qu'on se conditionne mentalement à l'être.

ABRAHAM LINCOLN (1809-1865)

16th President of the United States of America
16° Presidente de los Estados Unidos de América
16ᵉ Président des États-Unis d'Amérique

Since everything around you is always changing, to succeed you have to stay out in front of those changes.

ଚୠଓଃ

Ya que todo está siempre cambiando a su alrededor, para triunfar usted tiene que adelantarse a estos cambios.

ଚୠଓଃ

Comme le monde change constamment autour de nous il faut, pour réussir, se tenir à l'avant-garde de ces changements.

SAM M. WALTON (1918-1992)

American Entrepreneur, Founder of Wal-Mart
Hombre de Negocios Americano, Fundador de las Empresas
Wal-Mart
Homme d'affaires américain, Fondateur des Entreprises Wal-Mart

April 25
25 de abril
25 avril

The world is your kaleidoscope, and the varying combinations of colors which at every succeeding moment it presents to you are the exquisitely adjusted pictures of your ever-moving thoughts.

ಬಂದ

El mundo es nuestro kaleidoscopio y las variedades de combinaciones de colores que se presentan en cada instante son las imágenes bien arregladas de cada uno de nuestros pensamientos.

ಬಂದ

Le monde est notre kaléidoscope et les diverses combinaisons de couleurs qu'il nous présente à chaque instant nous révèlent des images précises de nos pensées qui changent continuellement.

JAMES ALLEN (1864-1912)

English Writer, Author of the book *As a Man Thinketh*
Escritor Inglés, Autor del libro *As a Man Thinketh*
Écrivain anglais, auteur du livre *As a Man Thinketh*

A free man is not envious; he naturally admits the existence of greatness and feels happy that such thing exists.

৪৩৫৪

El hombre libre no es envidioso; admite de buenas ganas lo que es grande y goza de disfrutar de que estas cosas ocurran.

৪৩৫৪

L'homme libre n'est point envieux; il admet volontiers ce qui est grand et se réjouit que cela puisse exister.

FRIEDRICH HEGEL (1770-1831)

German Philosopher
Filósofo Alemán
Philosophe allemande

April 27
27 de abril
27 avril

Good humor is the health of the soul, sadness its poison.

&OCB

El buen humor es la salud del alma; la tristeza es su veneno.

&OCB

La bonne humeur est la santé de l'âme; la tristesse, son poison.

ANONYMOUS
ANONIMO
ANONYME

One of the things I keep learning is that the secret of being happy is doing things for other people.

৪০৪

Una de las cosas que sigo aprendiendo es que el secreto de la felicidad está en hacer cosas para los demás.

৪০৪

Une des choses que j'apprends sans cesse est que le secret du bonheur c'est de servir les autres.

DICK GREGORY (b. 1932)

American Civic Leader
Líder Cívico Americano
Leader civique américain

April 29
29 de abril
29 avril

To a father the cheer of a life of accomplishments and to an educator the satisfaction of a job well done. But there is always a noble influence in any spiritual education and the most active, the most constant, the most productive is the one that flows from the loving heart of a mother.

⊱⊰

Queda al padre el consuelo de haber cumplido como bueno; queda al maestro la convicción de su deber. Pero en toda formación espiritual hay una noble influencia; y la más activa, la más continua, la más bienhechora es la que emana del corazón amoroso de la madre.

⊱⊰

Au père revient le mérite d'une vie pleine de réalisations; à l'éducateur, la satisfaction du devoir accompli. Cependant, dans toute éducation spirituelle s'exerce toujours une noble influence; la plus forte, la plus constante, la plus productive est celle qui jaillit du coeur rempli d'amour d'une mère.

EUGENIO MARÍA DE HOSTOS (1839-1903)

Puerto Rican Educator, Writer & Journalist
Educador, Escritor & Periodista Puertorriqueño
Educateur, écrivain et journalist portoricain

April 30
30 de abril
30 avril

Education is a lifelong process of which schooling is only a small but necessary part. As long as one remains alive and healthy, learning can go on — and should. But mental, moral, and spiritual growth can go on and should go on for a lifetime.

൭൦ഗ

La educación es un proceso que dura toda la vida y la enseñanza preparatoria es solamente una parte pequeña pero necesaria. Mientras continuemos con vida, en buena salud, podemos - y debemos - continuar aprendiendo. El crecimiento mental, moral y espiritual puede y debe continuar por toda la vida.

൭൦ഗ

L'éducation est un travail permanent dont l'école représente une faible mais indispensable partie. Tant qu'on est vivant et en santé, on peut et on doit continuer à étudier. La croissance spirituelle, morale et civique doit continuer toute la vie.

MORTIMER J. ADLER (1902-2000)

American Educator, Author of *The Paideia Proposal*
Educador Americano, Autor de *The Paideia Proposal*
Éducateur américain, auteur de *The Paideia Proposal*

MAY—MAYO—MAI

1 . . . . .GEORGE BERNARD SHAW
2 . . . . .ALBERT CAMUS
3 . . . . .JAMES CASH PENNEY

4 . . . . .RICHARD GERE
5 . . . . .DALAI LAMA
6 . . . . .ANONYMOUS

7 . . . . .INÉS M. MENDOZA
8 . . . . .EDOUARD F. LAFONTANT
9 . . . . .MA. ROBINSON

10 . . . . .JOHANN WOLFGANG GOETHE
11 . . . . .ANDREW YOUNG
12 . . . . .STEVEN SPIELBERG

13 . . . . .JOHN STEINBECK
14 . . . . .VICTOR HUGO
15 . . . . .MARTIN LUTHER KING JR.

16 . . . . .JAWAHARLAL NEHRU
17 . . . . .JOHN WOODEN
18 . . . . .HENRY FORD

19 . . . . .MOHONDAS "MAHATMA" GANDHI
20 . . . . .DOUGLAS MAC ARTHUR
21 . . . . .SIMÓN BOLÍVAR

22 . . . . .KAROL WOJTYLA, POPE JOHN
                                               PAUL II
23 . . . . .ANONYMOUS
24 . . . . .JAMES ALLEN

25 . . . . .RICHARD BACH
26 . . . . .THE BIBLE
27 . . . . .SWEDISH PROVERB

28 . . . . .SAI BABA
29 . . . . .ERIC FROMM
30 . . . . .PAUL J. MEYER
31 . . . . .RALPH WALDO EMERSON

May 1
1 de mayo
1er mai

Tired of Working? The year is made up of 365 days, each having 24 hours, 12 of which are nighttime hours, which add up to a total of 182 days. This leaves you with 183 days to work minus 52 Saturdays, which leaves you with 131 days to work minus 52 Sundays, which leaves you with 79 days to work.

But, there are 4 hours each day, set aside for eating, which adds up to 60 days, which leaves you 19 days for working. But you are entitled to 15 days of vacation, which means you have 4 days left for work minus 3 days, which you usually take off due to illness, which leaves you 1 day to work, which happens to be LABOR DAY[1], which is a holiday. So, why are you so tired?

ನಿಂದ

¿Cansado de trabajar? Recuerde, el año tiene 365 días, de los cuales 12 horas diarias están dedicadas a dormir y sumadas harían un total de 182 días. Por lo tanto, quedarían 183 días de trabajo, menos 52 sábados, quedarían 131 días, menos 52 domingos, quedarían 79 días de trabajo al año.

Pero hay 4 horas diarias dedicadas a la comida, que sumadas harían un total de 60 días; por lo tanto, quedarían 19 días de trabajo, menos 15 días de vacaciones a que usted tiene derecho, quedarían 4 días de trabajo. Si usted se enferma 3 veces al año y no trabaja, quedaría 1 día de trabajo. Pero ese día precisamente es el DIA DEL TRABAJO (1ro. de mayo), en el cual no se trabaja porque es día feriado. Entonces, ¿de qué está cansado usted?

---

1. In the USA, Labor Day is a different day each year in early September.

Fatigué de travailler? Considère ceci: Une année compte 365 jours. Tu passes 12 heures par jour à dormir, soit 182 jours. Il te reste alors 183 jours, enlève 52 samedis et 52 dimanches, il ne te reste que 79 jours de travail.

Mais tu consacres 4 heures par jour au manger soit 60 jours et tu as droit à 15 jours de vacances, il ne te reste alors que 4 jours de travail. Si tu prends alors 3 jours de congé maladie, il ne te restera qu'un seul jour de travail. Précisément, ce jour-là (1er. Mai), personne ne travaille car c'est un jour férié. Alors! Qu'est-ce qui te fatigue?

GEORGE BERNARD SHAW (1856-1950)

Irish Playwright
Dramaturgo Irlandés
Dramaturge irlandais

May 2
2 de mayo
2 mai

People forgive your happiness and your success only if you consent to share generously with them.

৩০০৪

La gente perdonará su felicidad y sus éxitos solamente si usted acepta a compartir generosamente con ellos.

৩০০৪

Les gens vous pardonnent votre bonheur et vos succès si vous consentez à les partager généreusement avec eux.

ALBERT CAMUS (1913-1960)

French Writer
Escritor Francés
Écrivain français

Give me a stock clerk with a goal, and I will give you a man who will make history. Give me a man without a goal, and I will give you a stock clerk.

೫೦೦೪

Dáme un dependiente con una meta y te daré un hombre que hará historia. Dáme un hombre sin una meta y te daré un dependiente.

೫೦೦೪

Donnez-moi un commis avec un but et je vous donnerai un homme qui fera l'histoire. Donnez-moi un homme sans but, je vous donnerai un commis.

JAMES CASH PENNEY (1875-1971)

American Entrepreneur, Founder of J. C. Penney's
Hombre de Negocios Americano, Fundador de J. C. Penney's
Homme d'affaires américain, fondateur des Entreprises J. C. Penney's

May 4
4 de mayo
4 mai

We cannot live according to what people expect from us; doing it would be like dying slowly every day.

ಬಿಂಜ

No debemos vivir según lo que se espera de nosotros; hacerlo sería una pequeña muerte diaria.

ಬಿಂಜ

Nous ne pouvons pas vivre d'après ce que les autres attendent de nous; vivre ainsi, c'est mourir lentement jour après jour.

RICHARD GERE (b. 1949)

American Actor
Actor Americano
Acteur américain

Ideals are the engine of progress . . . if we observe the evolution of human society, we will see the need for a vision to spark positive changes.

৪৩০৪

Los ideales son los generadores del progreso . . . si miramos la evolución de la sociedad humana, vemos la necesidad de tener visión para provocar cambios positivos.

৪৩০৪

Les rêves sont les moteurs du progrès . . . si nous observons l'évolution de la societé humaine, nous verrons la nécessité d'une vision pour provoquer des changements positifs.

TENZIN GYATSO, 14ᵗʰ DALAI LAMA (b. 1935)

Spiritual Leader of Tibet
Lider Espiritual del Tibet
Leader spirituel du Tibet

May 6
6 de mayo
6 mai

When there is a hill to climb, don't think that waiting will make it less steep.

ഇൗങ്ങ

Si hay que escalar una montaña, esperar para hacerlo no hará que la montaña se achique.

ഇൗങ്ങ

Quand il y a une montagne à escalader, ne pensez pas que le fait d'attendre la rendra moins escarpée.

ANONYMOUS
ANONIMO
ANONYME

Puerto Rico needs people that can reach "the new dawn."

৪৩৫৪

Puerto Rico necesita de hombres que puedan alcanzar "la nueva aurora".

৪৩৫৪

Porto Rico a besoin d'hommes capables d'atteindre "la nouvelle aurore".

INÉS M. MENDOZA (1908-1990)

Wife of Luis Muñoz Marín, First Elected Puerto Rican Governor
Esposa de Luis Muñoz Marín, 1ᵉʳ Gobernador Electo de Puerto Rico
Épouse de Luis Muñoz Marín, Premier Gouverneur élu de
Porto Rico

May 8
8 de mayo
8 mai

Leadership is the ability to profit from our multiple intelligences in order to transform our dreams into realities.

೫೦೧೪

El liderato es la habilidad de aprovechar las múltiples inteligencias que tenemos para convertir nuestros sueños en realidades.

೫೦೧೪

Le leadership est la faculté de profiter de nos multiples intelligences pour concrétiser nos rêves.

EDOUARD F. LAFONTANT (b. 1932)

Master Motivator
Maestro Motivador
Maître motivateur

Nobody can go back and start a new beginning, but anyone can start today to forge for himself a new destiny.

୫୦୯ଓ

Nadie puede retroceder y comenzar de nuevo, pero cada persona puede empezar hoy a forjarse un nuevo destino.

୫୦୯ଓ

Personne ne peut effacer son passé et recommencer; mais n'importe qui peut commencer dès aujourd'hui à se forger un nouveau destin.

MA. ROBINSON (1758-1800)

English Actress & Writer
Actriz & Escritora Inglesa
Actrice et écrivaine anglaise

May 10
10 de mayo
10 mai

Our dreams are our secret treasures, preludes of what we will do later.

ဆာ၈

Nuestros sueños son nuestros tesoros escondidos, preludios de lo que haremos más tarde.

ဆာ၈

Nos rêves sont nos trésors cachés, les préludes de nos actions futures.

JOHANN WOLFGANG GOETHE (1749-1832)

German Poet & Writer
Poeta & Escritor Alemán
Poète et écrivain allemand

God, I am so grateful to be the Mayor of this city, fifteen years ago I was put in jail by the order of the Mayor.

ဆာလ

¡Dios, cuán agradecido estoy de ser Alcalde de esta ciudad hoy! Hace quince años atrás, fuí encarcelado por órdenes del Alcalde.

ဆာလ

Mon Dieu! Comme je te suis reconnaissant d'être le maire de cette ville aujourd'hui, cette même ville où j'ai été emprisonné il y a quinze ans par ordre du maire.

ANDREW YOUNG (b. 1932)

Former Mayor of the City of Atlanta (Georgia)
Ex Alcalde de la Ciudad de Atlanta (Georgia)
Ex-Maire de la ville d'Atlanta (Georgia)

May 12
12 de mayo
12 mai

I have six children, four with my wife Kara and two adopted. I do not remember who are the adopted ones.

ಬಂಗ

Tengo seis niños, cuatro con mi esposa Kara y dos que hemos adoptado. No recuerdo cuáles son los adoptados.

ಬಂಗ

J'ai six enfants, quatre de mon épouse Kara et deux adoptions. Je ne me rappelle pas lesquels sont les adoptés.

STEVEN SPIELBERG (b. 1946)

American Movie Director (In an interview with Larry King)
Director de Cine Americano (En una entrevista con Larry King)
Cinéaste américain (Entrevue avec Larry King)

The free, exploring mind of the individual human is the most valuable thing in the world.

⊱⊰

El espíritu libre y curioso del hombre es lo que más vale en el mundo.

⊱⊰

L'esprit libre et curieux de l'homme est ce qu'il y a de plus précieux au monde.

JOHN STEINBECK (1902-1968)

American Writer, Author of *East of Eden*
Escritor Americano, Autor de *East of Eden*
Écrivain américain, auteur de *East of Eden*

May 14
14 de mayo
14 mai

It is not our perseverance that motivates us to achieve a goal . . .
it is the importance of the goal that motivates us to persevere.

೮೦೦೪

No es la perseverancia la que nos hace alcanzar un empeño . . .
es la importancia del empeño lo que nos hace perseverar.

೮೦೦೪

Ce n'est pas la persévérance qui nous pousse à atteindre un but;
c'est l'importance du but qui nous incite à persévérer.

VICTOR HUGO (1802-1885)

French Writer
Escritor Francés
Écrivain français

May 15
15 de mayo
15 mai

There is nothing in all the world greater than freedom. I would rather be a free pauper than a rich slave.

ജരു

No hay nada en el mundo más grande que la libertad. Prefiero ser un pobre libre que un esclavo rico.

ജരു

Il n' y a rien de plus grand au monde que la liberté. Je préfère être un pauvre libre qu'un esclave riche.

MARTIN LUTHER KING JR. (1929-1968)

American Civil Rights Leader
Líder de Derechos Civiles Americano
Leader américain des Droits civils

May 16
16 de mayo
16 mai

Teach people that they are capable of becoming happier and more civilized on this earth, capable of becoming a true man, master of his fate and captain of his soul.

৪৩৫৪

Enseña al prójimo que es capaz de ser más feliz y más civilizado, en esta tierra, capaz de convertirse en verdadero hombre, dueño de su destino y capitán de su alma.

৪৩৫৪

Enseigne à ton prochain qu'il est capable d'être plus heureux et plus civilisé sur cette terre; capable de devenir un homme accompli, c'est-à-dire maître de son destin et guide de son âme.

JAWAHARLAL NEHRU (1889-1964)

India's Prime Minister in 1947
Primer Ministro de la India en 1947
Premier ministre indien 1947

Do not let what you cannot do interfere with what you can do.

৪০৫৪

No deje que lo que usted no puede hacer interfiera con lo que usted puede hacer.

৪০৫৪

N' acceptez pas que les difficultés paralysent votre action.

JOHN WOODEN (b. 1910)

Basketball Coach & Motivator
Entrenador de Baloncesto y Motivador Americano
Entraîneur de basket-ball et motivateur américain

May 18
18 de mayo
18 mai

It is not the employer who pays wages—he only handles the money. It is the product that pays wages.

ຂວຉ

No es el patrono el que paga los salarios, solamente él se lo entrega. Es el producto el que paga los salarios.

ຂວຉ

Ce n'est pas l'employeur qui paie les salaires - il gère l'argent. C'est le produit qui paie les salaires.

HENRY FORD (1863-1947)

American Industrialist
Founder of the Ford Motor Company
Industrial Americano
Fundador de la Ford Motor Company
Industriel américain
Fondateur de Ford Motor Company

May 19
19 de mayo
19 mai

The only tyrant I accept in this world is the still voice within.

୫୬୯

El único tirano que acepto en este mundo es esta silenciosa voz interna.

୫୬୯

L'unique tyrannie que j'accepte en ce monde est celle de ma conscience.

MOHONDAS "MAHATMA" GANDHI (1869-1948)

Indian Political & Religious Leader
Líder Político & Religioso Indio
Leader politique et religieux indien

May 20
20 de mayo
20 mai

Build me a son, O Lord, who will be strong enough to know when he is weak, and brave enough to face himself when he is afraid, one who will be proud and unbending in honest defeat, and humble and gentle in victory.

୫୬ୠ୫

Dáme un hijo, Oh Señor!, que sea suficientemente fuerte para saber cuando él es débil y suficiente valiente para hacer frente a sí mismo cuando tiene miedo, un hijo que sea orgulloso e inflexible en la derrota y humilde y gentil en la victoria.

୫୬ୠ୫

Donne-moi, O Seigneur, un fils qui serait assez fort pour connaître ses faiblesses et assez brave pour résister quand il a peur, un fils qui serait fier et inflexible dans la défaite, humble et doux dans la victoire.

DOUGLAS MAC ARTHUR (1880-1964)

American General
General Americano
Général américain

He who does not expect to win is already defeated.

❧☙

¡Quien no espera vencer, ya está vencido!

❧☙

Celui qui n'attend pas la victoire est déjà vaincu.

SIMÓN BOLÍVAR (1783-1830)

Venezuelan General & Statesman
General & Estadista Venezolano
Général et homme d'État vénézuélien

May 22
22 de mayo
22 mai

To raise a joyful family requires a lot of cooperation between parents and children. Each member of the family has to be, in a special way, the servant of the others.

ജ൬രു

Para mantener una familia alegre, se requiere mucho, tanto de los padres como de los hijos. Cada miembro de la familia debe ser, de manera especial, el servidor de los demás.

ജ൬രു

Pour élever une famille dans la joie, il faut beaucoup de coopération entre parents et enfants. Chaque membre de la famille doit être, d'une manière spéciale, le serviteur des autres membres de la famille.

KAROL WOJTYLA (b. 1920)

Pope John Paul II
Papa Juan Pablo II
Pape Jean Paul II

With the passing of the years, it appears to me that what makes life so beautiful is love, grace, tenderness; it is not ingeniousness, intelligence or the greatness of knowledge—no matter how important it might be. It is the laughter of the children, the relationship with friends, the delightful conversations by the fire, the beauty of the flowers, the sound of music.

ഹെൻ

Lo que me parece que vuelve más bella la vida a medida que pasa es el amor, la gracia y la ternura; no el ingenio, ni la inteligencia, ni la grandeza del saber - por importante que sea - , sino sencillamente las risas de los niños, el trato con los amigos, las agradables charlas junto al fuego, la belleza de las flores y el sonido de la música.

ഹെൻ

Il me semble que - au fil des années - ce qui rend la vie plus belle c'est l'amour, la grâce et la tendresse. Ce n'est ni l'ingéniosité, ni l'intelligence, ni l'étendue du savoir - quelle que soit son importance - c'est simplement le rire des enfants, les relations avec les amis, les agréables conversations autour du feu, la beauté des fleurs et le son de la musique.

ANONYMOUS
ANONIMO
ANONYME

May 24
24 de mayo
24 mai

Man is the master of thought, the moulder of character, and the maker and shaper of condition, environment, and destiny.

୫୦୧ଓ

El hombre es un maestro del pensamiento, un escultor de personalidad, un creador y forjador de los eventos, del medio ambiente y del destino.

୫୦୧ଓ

L'homme est un maître à penser, un sculpteur de personnalité, un créateur et contrôleur d'événements, d'environnement et de destin.

JAMES ALLEN (1864-1912)

English Writer, Author of the book *As a Man Thinketh*
Escritor Inglés, Autor del libro *As a Man Thinketh*
Écrivain anglais, auteur du livre *As a Man Thinketh*

Dream what you can dare to dream,
Go where you want to go,
Be what you want to be,
Live!

ॐ

Sueñe lo que usted se atreva a soñar,
Vaya donde usted quiera ir,
Sea lo que usted quiera ser,
¡Viva!

ॐ

Osez avoir les rêves les plus fous,
Allez où vous voulez,
Soyez ce que vous voulez devenir,
Vivez!

RICHARD BACH (b. 1936)

American Writer, Author of *Jonathan Livingston Seagull*
Escritor Americano, Autor de *Juan Salvador Gaviota*
Écrivain américain, auteur de *Jonathan Livingston Seagull*

May 26
26 de mayo
26 mai

Give and it will be given unto you — good measure pressed down — shaken together — for with the measure you use it will be measured to you.

ଔ୯ଓ

Den, y se les dará; recibirán una medida bien llena, apretada y rebosante; porque, con la medida que ustedes midan, serán medidos.

ଔ୯ଓ

Donnez, et on vous donnera une bonne mesure, pressée, tassée, débordante; car c'est avec la mesure que vous employez qu'en retour on mesurera pour vous.

THE BIBLE – LA BIBLIA – LA BIBLE

St. Luke 6:38
San Lucas 6:38
St. Luc 6:38

May 27
27 de mayo
27 mai

Shared joy is double joy; shared pain is half pain.

৪০০৪

Alegría compartida es alegría doble; tristeza compartida es media tristeza.

৪০০৪

Joie partagée, joie doublée. Peine partagée, peine à moitié.

SWEDISH PROVERB
PROVERBIO SUECO
PROVERBE SUÉDOIS

May 28
28 de mayo
28 mai

No joy matches the one we get when we serve others.

ৰেত্তও

Ninguna alegría iguala el gozo de servir a los demás.

ৰেত্তও

Aucune joie n'égale celle de servir autrui.

SAI BABA

Indian Spiritual Leader
Líder Espiritual Indio
Leader spirituel indien

The true rich is not the one who has a lot, but the one who gives a lot.

కుౕన

El verdadero rico no es el que tiene mucho, es el que dá mucho.

కుౕన

Le vrai riche n'est pas celui qui possède beaucoup, mais celui qui donne beaucoup.

ERIC FROMM (1900-1980)

German-American Psychoanalyst
Sicoanalista Germano-Americano
Psychanalyste germano-américain

May 30
30 de mayo
30 mai

Every great religion, philosophy, invention or work of art had its creative beginning in the mind of one person with desire.

☙ℭ঩

Todas las religiones, los sistemas filosóficos, los inventos y las obras de arte tuvieron su principio creativo en la mente de una persona motivada.

☙ℭ঩

Toutes les grandes religions, les systèmes philosophiques, les inventions et oeuvres d'art ont pris naissance dans l'esprit d'une personne motivée.

PAUL J. MEYER (b. 1928)

American Entrepreneur & Educator
Founder of the Success Motivation Institute's Companies
Empresario & Educador Americano
Fundador de las Empresas Success Motivation Institute
Homme d'affaires et éducateur américain
Fondateur des Entreprises Success Motivation Institue

God offers to every mind a choice between truth and repose.
Take which you please—you can never have both.

⊱⊰

Dios ofrece a cada mente una elección entre la verdad y la
quietud. Escoja lo que le plazca - usted nunca puede tener las
dos.

⊱⊰

Dieu offre à chaque esprit un choix entre la recherche de la vérité
et la tranquillité d'esprit; choisissez la voie qui vous plaît car
vous ne pouvez pas avoir les deux.

RALPH WALDO EMERSON (1803-1882)

American Philosopher, Poet & Essayist
Filósofo, Poeta & Ensayista Americano
Philosophe, poète et essayiste américain

JUNE — JUNIO — JUIN

1 ....THE BIBLE
2 ....JOHN KASPAR LAVATER
3 ....PLATO

4 ....ABRAHAM LINCOLN
5 ....WILL ROGERS
6 ....BENJAMIN FRANKLIN

7 ....SAM M. WALTON
8 ....BLAISE PASCAL
9 ....MAO TSE TUNG

10 ....PAUL J. MEYER
11 ....EDOUARD F. LAFONTANT
12 ....JAMES JOYCE

13 ....ALBERT EINSTEIN
14 ....ERNESTO "CHE" GUEVARA
15 ....NAPOLÉON BONAPARTE

16 ....PYTHAGORAS
17 ....RALPH WALDO EMERSON
18 ....HAROLD MCMILLAN

19 ....DALAI LAMA
20 ....OG MANDINO
21 ....JULES HENRI POINCARRÉ

22 ....BENJAMIN DISRAELI
23 ....THOMAS JEFFERSON
24 ....HORACE MANN

25 ....WM. SOMERSET MAUGHAM
26 ....SAMUEL JOHNSON
27 ....HENRY FORD

28 ....MOHONDAS "MAHATMA" GANDHI
29 ....ANONYMOUS
30 ....VICTOR HUGO

June 1
1 de junio
1ᵉʳ juin

If any man desires to be the first, the same shall be last of all, and servant of all.

ଈଠଔଓ

Quien quiera ser el primero, que sea el último de todos y el servidor de todos.

ଈଠଔଓ

Si quelqu'un veut être le premier, il doit être le dernier de tous et le serviteur de tous.

THE BIBLE — LA BIBLIA — LA BIBLE

St. Mark 9:35
San Marcos 9:35
Saint Marc 9:35

He who has never forgiven an enemy has never known one of the most sublime joys of life.

෨෮ଓ

El que no haya perdonado a un enemigo nunca ha conocido uno de los más sublimes gozos de la vida.

෨෮ଓ

Celui qui jamais n'a pardonné à un ennemi n'a jamais connu l'une des plus sublimes joies de la vie.

JOHN KASPAR LAVATER (1741-1801)

Swiss Philosopher
Filósofo Suizo
Philosophe suisse

June 3
3 de junio
3 juin

Every one of us has kings or slaves, barbarians or greeks as ancestors.

ଚ୨ଓ୪

Todo individuo tiene reyes o esclavos, bárbaros o griegos como ancestros.

ଚ୨ଓ୪

Tout individu a des rois ou des esclaves, des barbares ou des grecs comme ancêtres.

PLATO (427-347 B.C.)

Greek Philosopher
Filósofo Griego
Philosophe grec

If it were not for my little jokes, I could not bear the burden of this office.

❧⊰

Si no fuese por estos pequeños chistes míos, no podría soportar la carga de este trabajo.

❧⊰

Sans mes petites plaisanteries, je ne pourrais pas supporter le poids de la présidence.

ABRAHAM LINCOLN (1809-1865)

16th President of the United States of America
16º Presidente de los Estados Unidos de América
16e Président des États-Unis d'Amérique

June 5
5 de junio
5 juin

I don't make jokes. I just watch the government and report the facts.

✂

No hago chistes. Solamente observo al gobierno y digo los hechos.

✂

Je n'invente pas de blagues. J'observe le gouvernement et je rapporte les faits.

WILL ROGERS (1879-1935)

American Actor & Humorist
Actor & Humorista Americano
Acteur et humoriste américain

Joy is not in things, it is in us.

ཀའཀཚ

La alegría no se encuentra en las cosas; está en uno mismo.

ཀའཀཚ

La joie ne se trouve pas dans les choses; elle est en nous-mêmes.

BENJAMIN FRANKLIN (1706-1790)

American Statesman, Writer & Publicist
Hombre de Estado, Escritor & Publicista Americano
Homme d'État, écrivain et journaliste américain

June 7
7 de junio
7 juin

Making people want to come back . . . that's where the profits
come from . . . people coming back over and over again.

ಹಿಂ

Hacer que los clientes regresen . . . ahí es donde se encuentran
las ganancias . . . clientes que vuelven a nuestras tiendas una vez
y muchas veces más.

ಹಿಂ

Faire en sorte que les clients reviennent . . . Voilà où se trouvent
les profits . . . des clients qui reviennent sans cesse.

SAM M. WALTON (1918-1992)

American Entrepreneur, Founder of Wal-Mart Stores
Empresario Americano, Fundador de las Tiendas Wal-Mart
Homme d'affaires américain, Fondateur des Entreprises Wal-Mart

Know that man surpasses man infinitely.

ഇറ്റ

Sabed que el hombre sobrepasa al hombre infinitamente.

ഇറ്റ

Apprenez que l'homme surpasse l'homme infiniment.

BLAISE PASCAL (1623-1662)

French Mathematician, Physicist, Philosopher & Writer
Matemático, Físico, Filósofo & Escritor Francés
Mathématicien, physicien, philosophe et écrivain français

June 9
9 de junio
9 juin

In difficult times, we always have to keep our successes in our mind, see our brilliant perspective and increase our courage.

৪০০৪

En tiempo difíciles, debemos tener presentes nuestros éxitos, ver nuestra brillante perspectiva y aumentar nuestro coraje.

৪০০৪

Dans les moments difficiles, nous devons penser à nos triomphes, visualiser nos brillantes perspectives et ainsi renforcer notre courage.

MAO TSE TUNG (1893-1976)

Chinese Political Leader
Líder Político Chino
Leader politique chinois

Every change in human attitude must come through internal understanding and acceptance. Human beings are the only known creatures who can reshape and remold themselves by altering their attitudes.

ঙ৩েৎ

Todo cambio de actitud debe provenir de una comprensión y una aceptación interna. El hombre es la única criatura conocida que puede reinventarse cambiando sus actitudes.

ঙ৩েৎ

Tout changement d'attitude doit naître d'une compréhension et d'une acceptation de soi. L'être humain est l'unique créature connue qui soit capable de se remodeler lui-même en changeant ses attitudes.

PAUL J. MEYER (b. 1928)

American Entrepreneur & Educator
Founder of The Success Motivation Institute's Companies
Empresario & Educador Americano
Fundador de las Empresas Success Motivation Institute
Homme d'affaires et éducateur américain
Fondateur des Entreprises Success Motivation Institute

June 11
11 de junio
11 juin

Henry David Thoreau wrote that the majority of people live in a state of **silent desperation**. Don't let this happen to you and don't let your life pass through your fingers like the sand of the beach through the fingers of a child.

⁂

Henry David Thoreau pensó que la mayoría de los hombres llevan una vida de **desesperanza muda**. No permita que esto le pase a usted y no deje que su vida pase por los dedos de su mano como la arena de la playa pasa por los dedos de los niños.

⁂

D'après Henry David Thoreau la majorité des hommes vivent dans un état de **désespoir muet**. N'acceptez pas un pareil sort et ne laissez pas couler votre vie comme le sable de la plage entre les doigts d'un enfant.

EDOUARD F. LAFONTANT (b. 1932)

Master Motivator
Maestro Motivador
Maître motivateur

June 12
12 de junio
12 juin

A man of genius makes no mistakes. His errors are volitional and are the portals of discovery.

⊗⊗

Una persona genial no comete errores. Sus errores son volitivos y abren las puertas de los descubrimientos.

⊗⊗

Un génie ne commet pas d'erreurs. Ses erreurs sont volitives et ouvrent la porte aux découvertes.

JAMES JOYCE (1882-1941)

Irish Writer
Escritor Irlandés
Écrivain irlandais

199

June 13
13 de junio
13 juin

Whoever is careless with the truth in small matters cannot be trusted with important matters.

ಬೋಥ

A los que son descuidados con la verdad en asuntos pequeños no se les puede tener confianza en asuntos importantes.

ಬೋಥ

Dans les affaires importantes, on ne peut pas avoir confiance en ceux qui prennent la vérité à la légère dans les affaires courantes.

ALBERT EINSTEIN (1879-1955)

German-American Scientist
Científico Germano-Americano
Scientifique américain d'origine allemande

When the destiny of the human race is at stake, the dangers or the sacrifices of a man or a country do not matter.

ാറ

Qué importan los peligros o sacrificios de un hombre o de un pueblo cuando está en juego el destino de la humanidad.

ാറ

Peu importent les dangers ou les sacrifices d'un homme ou d'un peuple quand l'enjeu est le destin de l' humanité.

ERNESTO "CHE" GUEVARA (1928-1967)

Argentinean-Cuban Politician & Doctor
Político & Médico Argentino-Cubano
Homme politique et médecin cubain d'origine argentine

June 15
15 de junio
15 juin

A head without memory is just like a fortress without soldiers.

જીજ્ઝ

Una cabeza sin memoria es como una fortaleza sin guarnición.

જીજ્ઝ

Une tête sans mémoire est comme une citadelle sans soldats.

NAPOLÉON BONAPARTE (1769-1821)

Emperor of France (1804-1815)
Emperador de Francia (1804-1815)
Empereur de France (1804-1815)

The two oldest and shortest words—yes and no—are those which require the most thinking.

৪১০৪৪

Las palabras más antiguas y más cortas - sí y no - son las que requieren más pensamiento.

৪১০৪৪

Les mots les plus anciens et les plus courts - oui et non - sont ceux qui demandent le plus de réflexion.

PYTHAGORAS (c. 580-500 B.C.)

Greek Philosopher & Mathematician
Filósofo & Matemático Griego
Philosophe et mathématicien grec

June 17
17 de junio
17 juin

Life is not so short that there is not always time enough for courtesy.

৪৩৬৪

La vida no es tan corta para que crea que no hay suficiente tiempo para la cortesía.

৪৩৬৪

La vie n'est pas si courte qu'elle ne laisse pas assez de temps pour la courtoisie.

RALPH WALDO EMERSON (1803-1882)

American Philosopher
Filósofo Americano
Philosophe américain

Tradition does not mean that the living are dead; it means that the dead are living.

ఴింౚ

La tradición no quiere decir que los vivos estén muertos; significa que los muertos viven.

ఴింౚ

Tradition ne veut pas dire que les vivants sont morts; cela veut dire que les morts vivent.

HAROLD MCMILLAN (1894-1986)

British Prime Minister
Primer Ministro Británico
Premier Ministre britannique

June 19
19 de junio
19 juin

It is essential to address directly our tendency to put things off and while away our time in meaningless activities and from the challenge of transforming our habits on the ground that it is too great a task.

೦೦೮೩

Es imperativo prestar atención seriamente a nuestra tendencia de posponer ciertas metas y malgastar nuestro tiempo en actividades de poca importancia, evitando así el reto de transformar nuestros hábitos con la excusa que la tarea es demasiado grande.

೦೦೮೩

Il est urgent de corriger notre tendance à remettre à plus tard certaines décisions et à gaspiller notre temps dans des activités futiles et ainsi fuir le défi de changer nos habitudes sous prétexte que pareille tâche est trop difficile.

TENSIN GYATSO, 14th DALAI LAMA (b. 1935)

Spiritual Leader of Tibet
Líder Espiritual del Tibet
Leader spirituel du Tibet

SALESMAN'S PRAYER

Oh, Creator of all things, help me.

For this day I go out into the world
naked and alone, and without your
hand to guide me I will wander far
from the path which leads to
success and happiness.

Assign me tasks to which others have
failed; yet guide me to pluck the seeds
of success from their failures.

Confront me with fears that will temper
my spirit; yet endow me with courage
to laugh at my misgivings.

Help this humble salesman.
Guide me, God.

OG MANDINO (1923-1996)

American Motivator
Author of *The Greatest Salesman in the World*

ORACION DEL VENDEDOR

¡Oh, Creador de todas las cosas,
Ayúdame!

Hoy iré al mundo solo y
desamparado y si tu mano
no me guía, andaré lejos del
camino que conduce al triunfo
y la felicidad.

Dáme tareas donde otros han
fracasado, pero guíame para
hallar en sus derrotas las
semillas del éxito.

Confróntame con los temores
que fortalecerán mi espíritu,
pero dáme el valor de reirme
de mis temores.

Ayuda, ¡Oh, Señor!, a este
humilde vendedor.

OG MANDINO (1923-1996)

Motivador Americano
Autor del Libro *El Vendedor Más Grande del Mundo*

PRIÈRE DU VENDEUR

O Créateur de l'Univers,
Aide-moi!
Aujourd'hui, je m'engage dans les activités de ce monde
impuissant et seul.
Sans ta main pour me guider
je m'écarterai loin du sentier
qui mène à la réussite et au bonheur.

Assigne-moi des tâches ou d'autres
ont échoué, mais aide-moi à trouver
dans leurs échecs les semences de ma réussite.

Mets-moi en face de situations difficiles
pour fortifier mon esprit;
mais donne-moi aussi le courage
de rire de mes appréhensions.

Aide cet humble vendeur,
Sois mon guide, O Seigneur!

OG MANDINO (1923-1996)

Motivateur américain
Auteur du livre *Le Plus Grand Vendeur du Monde*

June 21
21 de junio
21 juin

Science is facts. Just as houses are made of stones, so is science made of facts. But a pile of stones is not a house and a collection of facts is not necessarily science.

&⚬ଔ

La ciencia es un conjunto de datos. Del mismo modo que las casas son hechas de piedras, la ciencia está hecha de datos. Sin embargo, una pila de piedras no es una casa y una colección de datos no es necesariamente ciencia.

&⚬ଔ

La science est faite de données. De même que les maisons sont faites de pierres, la science est faite de données. Cependant, une pile de pierres n'est pas une maison et une collection de données n'est pas nécessairement de la science.

JULES HENRI POINCARRÉ (1854-1912)

French Mathematician
Matemático Francés
Mathématicien français

June 22
22 de junio
22 juin

The greatest good you can do for another is not just to share your riches, but to reveal to him his own riches.

෨෬

El bien más grande que usted puede hacer a los demás no es solamente compartir sus riquezas, sino revelar a ellos sus propias riquezas.

෨෬

Le plus grand bien que vous puissiez faire à un autre ne consiste pas seulement à partager vos richesses avec lui mais à lui révéler ses propres richesses.

BENJAMIN DISRAELI (1804-1881)

British Prime Minister (1868-1874)
Primer Ministro Británico (1868-1874)
Premier Ministre britannique (1868-1874)

June 23
23 de junio
23 juin

When a man assumes a public trust, he should consider himself public property.

෴

Cuando una persona ocupa una posición pública de confianza, debería considerarse una propiedad pública.

෴

Quand une personne assume une responsabilité publique, il doit se considérer propriété publique.

THOMAS JEFFERSON (1743-1826)

3rd President of the United States of America
3° Presidente de los Estados Unidos de América
3e Président des États-Unis d'Amérique

Be ashamed to die until you have won some victory for humanity.

୫୬

Ten verguenza de morir hasta que hayas obtenido alguna victoria para la humanidad.

୫୬

Aie honte de mourir tant que tu n'as pas remporté quelque victoire pour l'humanité.

HORACE MANN (1796-1859)

American Educator
Educador Americano
Éducateur américain

June 25
25 de junio
25 juin

The great tragedy of life is not that men perish but that they cease to love.

જીલ્ડઝ

La grande tragedia de la vida no es que perezcan los seres humanos, sino que dejen de amar.

જીલ્ડઝ

La grande tragédie de la vie n'est pas que des hommes meurent, mais qu'ils cessent d'aimer.

WILLIAM SOMERSET MAUGHAM (1874-1965)

British Writer
Escritor Británico
Écrivain britannique

Curiosity is one of the permanent and certain characteristics of a vigorous intellect.

&⅋⅍

La curiosidad es una de las características permanentes y certeras de un intelecto vigoroso.

&⅋⅍

La curiosité est une des caractéristiques permanentes et évidentes d'un intellect solide.

SAMUEL JOHNSON (1709-1784)

English Lexicographer
Lexicógrafo Inglés
Lexicographe anglais

June 27
27 de junio
27 juin

Only when things are produced in quantity at the lowest cost and of the best quality and sold at the narrowest margin of profit, can we hope for real prosperity.

ഌരു

Solamente cuando unos productos son fabricados en cantidades, al costo más bajo y de la mejor calidad y pueden ser vendidos con el márgen de ganancia más estrecho, uno puede esperar verdadera prosperidad.

ഌരു

C'est seulement quand on fabrique des produits en grande quantité, au plus bas prix de revient et de la meilleure qualité, et qu'on les vend avec la marge de bénéfices la plus étroite qu' une véritable prospérité est possible.

HENRY FORD (1863-1947)

American Industrialist, Founder of the Ford Motor Company
Industrial Americano, Fundador de Ford Motor Company
Industriel américain, fondateur de la Ford Motor Company

Kindness is irresistible, providing it is heartfelt and sincere. For what can the most unprincipled of men do to you if you persist in being kind to him?

๏ช๛

La gentileza es irresistible, particularmente cuando es cordial y sincera. ¿Qué puede hacer el más inescrupuloso de los hombres frente al que persiste en su gentileza hacia él?

๏ช๛

La courtoisie est irrésistible, pourvu qu'elle soit naturelle et spontanée. Que peut faire le plus grossier personnage en face de celui qui ne lui témoigne que de la courtoisie?

MOHONDAS "MAHATMA" GANDHI (1869–1948)

Indian Political & Religious Leader
Líder Político & Religioso Indio
Leader politique et religieux indien

June 29
29 de junio
29 juin

People spend the first half of their lives destroying their health and the other half trying to restore it.

᠍᠍ৎৎ

El hombre pasa la primera mitad de su vida estropeándose su salud, y la segunda mitad tratando de curarse.

᠍᠍ৎৎ

L'homme passe la première moitié de sa vie à détruire sa santé et l'autre moitié à essayer de la rétablir.

ANONYMOUS
ANONIMO
ANONYME

Genius is God's manifestation on earth. In each masterpiece, we see the hand of God; each masterpiece is sort of a miracle.

৪০০৪

El genio en la tierra es Dios que se manifiesta. Cada vez que surge una obra maestra es una manifestación divina. Una obra maestra es una especie de milagro.

৪০০৪

Le génie est la manifestation de Dieu sur la terre. Dans chaque chef-d'oeuvre, on voit la main divine. Un chef-d'oeuvre est une sorte de miracle.

VICTOR HUGO (1802-1885)

French Writer
Escritor Francés
Écrivain français

JULY – JULIO – JUILLET

1 . . . . .AFRICAN LEGEND
2 . . . . .MOHONDAS "MAHATMA" GANDHI
3 . . . . .MAX DUPRÉE

4 . . . . .GEORGE WASHINGTON
5 . . . . .EDOUARD F. LAFONTANT
6 . . . . .MIGUEL DE CERVANTES SAAVEDRA

7 . . . . .FRANÇOIS MARIE AROUET – dit
. . . . .VOLTAIRE
8 . . . . .LEO TOLSTOY
9 . . . . .JEAN DE LA FONTAINE

10 . . . . .BEN JONSON
11 . . . . .HELEN ADAMS KELLER
12 . . . . .ENEID ROUTTE GÓMEZ

13 . . . . .JOHANN WOLFGANG VON GOETHE
14 . . . . .GABRIELLE "COCO" CHANEL
15 . . . . .JOHN H. PETROLINI

16 . . . . .ANONYMOUS
17 . . . . .BENJAMIN FRANKLIN
18 . . . . .HENRY FORD

19 . . . . .ANDRÉ MALRAUX
20 . . . . .PAUL J. MEYER
21 . . . . .BETTER BUSINESS BUREAU

22 . . . . .VICTOR HUGO
23 . . . . .LLOYD DAVID WARD
24 . . . . .ARTHUR CONAN DOYLE

25 . . . . .THE BIBLE
26 . . . . .EDMUND BURKE
27 . . . . .ANONYMOUS

28 . . . . .ALBERT SCHWEITZER
29 . . . . .ALEXIS CARREL
30 . . . . .WINSTON CHURCHILL
31 . . . . .OLIVER WENDELL HOLMES

Every morning in Africa,
A gazelle wakes up,
It must outrun
The fastest lion
Or it will be killed.
Every morning in Africa,
A lion wakes up,
It must outrun the
Slowest gazelle or
It will starve.
It doesn't matter whether
You're a lion or a gazelle.
When the sun comes up,
You'd better be running.

AFRICAN LEGEND

John Deere's Advertising in "The Economist"

Cada mañana en Africa
Se despierta una gacela,
Tiene que correr más rápido
Que el león más rápido
Si no ella muere.
Cada mañana en Africa
Se despierta un león,
Tiene que correr más rápido
Que la gacela más lenta
Si no muere de hambre.
No importa si usted es
Un león o una gacela.
Cuando salga el sol,
Empiece a correr.

LEYENDA AFRICANA

Publicidad de John Deere en "The Economist"

1er juillet

Chaque matin en Afrique
Une gazelle à son réveil
Doit courir plus vite
Que le lion le plus rapide,
Sinon, elle meurt.
Chaque matin en Afrique
Un lion à son réveil
Doit courir plus vite
Que la gazelle la plus lente,
Sinon, il meurt de faim.
Peu importe que vous soyez
Lion ou gazelle,
Dès le lever du soleil,
Commencez à courir.

LEGENDE AFRICAINE

Publicité de John Deere dans "The Economist"

Your strength does not come from your physical power; it stems from an indomitable desire.

≈

La fuerza no viene de la capacidad física. Proviene de un deseo indomable.

≈

Votre force ne vient pas de votre capacité physique, mais d'un désir indomptable.

MOHONDAS "MAHATMA" GANDHI (1869-1948)

Indian Political & Religious Leader
Líder Político & Religioso Indio
Leader politique et religieux indien

July 3
3 de julio
3 juillet

We can't become what we need to be by remaining what we are.

∞∞∞

No podemos convertirnos en lo que necesitamos ser manteniéndonos como estamos.

∞∞∞

Nous ne pouvons pas devenir ce que nous voulons être en demeurant ce que nous sommes.

MAX DUPRÉE

American Writer
Escritor Americano
Écrivain américain

Liberty, when it begins to take root, is a plant of rapid growth.

ଧୀଓଔ

Libertad, cuando empieza a desarrollar sus raíces, es una planta que crece rápidamente.

ଧୀଓଔ

Quand elle commence à développer des racines, la liberté est une plante qui pousse très vite.

GEORGE WASHINGTON (1732-1799)

1st President of the United States of America
1er Presidente de los Estados Unidos
1er Président des Étas-Unis d'Amérique

July 5
5 de julio
5 juillet

By improving the personal value of your people you will certainly improve the net worth of your company and yours too.

ഇൗൽ

El mejoramiento del valor personal de cada miembro de su organización mejorará el valor de la organización y el suyo también.

ഇൗൽ

En améliorant la valeur personnelle de chaque membre de votre organisation, vous améliorez la valeur de votre organisation et la vôtre aussi.

EDOUARD F. LAFONTANT (b. 1932)

Master Motivator
Maestro Motivador
Maître motivateur

If you choose valor as an ideal and dream of accomplishing great things, there is no reason to envy those who have these qualities. The reason is that you inherit blue blood, but you acquire valor and acquired valor has an intrinsic value, blue blood does not.

❧〇❧

Si tomas por medio la virtud y tú aprecias de hacer hechos virtuosos, no hay para qué tener envidia a los que los tienen . . . porque la sangre se hereda y la virtud se adquiere, y la virtud vale por sí sola lo que la sangre no vale.

❧〇❧

Si tu choisis comme idéal le courage, si tu rêves d'accomplir des actions héroïques, point n'est besoin d'envier ceux qui possèdent ces qualités. Car, on hérite du sang noble, mais le courage s'acquiert. Le courage a une valeur intrinsèque, le sang noble aucune.

MIGUEL DE CERVANTES SAAVEDRA (1547-1616)

Spanish Novelist, Poet, Creator of *Don Quixote*
Novelista, Poeta Español, Creador de *Don Quijote*
Romancier, poète, créateur de *Don Quichotte*

Happiness is often the only thing that one can give without having it, and it is in giving it that you acquire it.

ဆဝင္သ

La felicidad es a menudo la única cosa que usted puede dar sin tenerla y es al darla que usted la obtiene.

ဆဝင္သ

Le bonheur est souvent la seule chose qu'on puisse donner sans l'avoir et c'est en le donnant qu'on l'acquiert.

FRANçOIS MARIE AROUET — dit VOLTAIRE (1694-1778)

French Writer
Escritor Francés
Écrivain français

Mankind cannot apprehend fully the complexities of life; however, the desire to find their causes is rooted in his soul.

୫୦୯ଓ

La mente humana no puede comprender completamente las complejidades de la vida, pero el deseo de encontrar sus causas está implantado en el alma del ser humano.

୫୦୯ଓ

L'homme ne peut pas appréhender toutes les complexités de la vie, cependant le désir d'en trouver les causes est implanté dans son âme.

LEO TOLSTOY (1828-1910)

Russian Writer
Escritor Ruso
Écrivain russe

July 9
9 de julio
9 juillet

By his work, one knows the workman.

৪৩৫৩

Por su obra se conoce al trabajador.

৪৩৫৩

C'est à l'oeuvre que l'on connaît l'ouvrier.

JEAN DE LA FONTAINE (1621-1695)

French Poet
Poeta Francés
Poète français

I know of no disease of the soul but ignorance.

෨෮෬

No conozco de ninguna otra enfermedad del alma que no sea la ignorancia.

෨෮෬

Je ne connais qu'une maladie de l'âme: l'ignorance.

BEN JONSON (1572-1637)

English Actor & Poet
Actor & Poeta Inglés
Acteur et poète anglais

July 11
11 de julio
11 juillet

No nation is wise enough to rule another.

❧☙

Ninguna nación es suficientemente sabia como para gobernar otra nación.

❧☙

Aucune nation n'est assez sage pour en gouverner une autre.

HELEN ADAMS KELLER (1880-1968)

American Author & Educator, Blind & Deaf
Autora & Educadora Americana, Sordomuda
Auteure et Éducatrice américaine, sourde-muette

Mrs. Ethel Ríos de Betancourt is a woman who turned generosity into an art. She leaves peace on her path.

৵৩

Doña Ethel Ríos de Betancourt es una mujer que ha transformado la generosidad en un arte. Ella deja paz en su camino.

৵৩

Mme Ethel Ríos de Betancourt est une femme qui a fait de la générosité un art. Elle sème la paix sur son chemin.

ENEID ROUTTE GÓMEZ (b. 1944)

Puerto Rican Journalist
Periodista Puertorriqueña
Journaliste portoricaine

July 13
13 de julio
13 juillet

One ought, every day at least, to hear a little song, read a good poem, see a fine picture and, if it were possible, to speak a few reasonable words.

৪০৫঩

Cada uno debe por lo menos cada día escuchar una canción, leer un poema, mirar una pintura, y si es posible, decir algunas palabras sensatas.

৪০৫঩

Chacun doit, chaque jour au moins, écouter une chanson, lire un poème, regarder une belle peinture, et si possible, dire quelques mots sensés.

JOHANN WOLFGANG VON GOETHE (1749-1832)

German Poet
Poeta Alemán
Poète allemand

When you are 20 years old, you have the face that nature gave you.
At 40, you have the face that life gave you.
At 60, you have the face you deserve.

∞☙

A los 20 años, usted tiene la cara que le ha dado la naturaleza.
A los 40 años, usted tiene la cara que le ha dado la vida.
A los 60 años, usted tiene la cara que se merece.

∞☙

A 20 ans, vous avez le visage que vous a donné la nature.
A 40 ans, vous avez le visage que vous a donné la vie.
A 60 ans, vous avez le visage que vous méritez.

GABRIELLE "COCO" CHANEL (1883-1971)

French Fashion Designer
Modista Francesa
Couturière française

July 15
15 de julio
15 juillet

We want everybody in the organization to spend part of each day improving their jobs.

୫୬ଓଷ

Queremos que todos en la organización inviertan parte de cada día de trabajo en mejorarse.

୫୬ଓଷ

Nous voulons que chaque membre de l'organisation consacre une partie de chaque journée à l'amélioration de son travail.

JOHN H. PETROLINI

Technology Director
Director Tecnológico
Directeur technologique
Teradyne

A financial manager must not steer a company away from risks . . . without risks, there are no dreams.

৪৩৫১

Un director de finanzas no debe guiar a su compañía lejos de los riesgos; es que sin riesgo, no hay sueños.

৪৩৫১

Un directeur des finances ne doit pas conduire sa compagnie sur une voie sans risques . . . sans risques, aucun rêve n'est possible.

ANONYMOUS
ANONIMO
ANONYME

July 17
17 de julio
17 juillet

Do you love life? Then do not squander time, for that is the stuff life is made of.

॰ఐॐ

¿Te gusta la vida? Pues no malgastes tu tiempo porque del tiempo está hecha la vida.

॰ఐॐ

Tu aimes la vie? Eh bien! ne gaspille pas ton temps, car le temps est la matière première de la vie.

BENJAMIN FRANKLIN (1706-1790)

American Politician, Writer, Inventor & Businessman
Político, Escritor, Inventor & Hombre de Negocios Americano
Politicien, écrivain, inventeur et homme d'affaires américain

Nothing is particularly hard if you divide it into small jobs.

৪৩৫৩

Ningún trabajo es realmente duro si se divide en pequeñas partes.

৪৩৫৩

Aucun travail n'est réellement difficile si vous le divisez en petites parties.

HENRY FORD (1863-1947)

Founder of Ford Motor Company
Fundador de Ford Motor Company
Fondateur de Ford Motor Company

July 19
19 de julio
19 juillet

Happiness is not in accomplishments. It is in the heart of those living them.

৪৩৪

La felicidad no está en los logros. Se encuentra en el corazón de los que los viven.

৪৩৪

Le bonheur n'est pas dans les événements. Il est dans le coeur de ceux qui les vivent.

ANDRÉ MALRAUX (1901-1976)

French Writer
Escritor Francés
Écrivain français

The common denominator for success is work. Without work, one loses the vision, the confidence and the determination to achieve.

૭૦૦ૐ

El común denominador del éxito es el trabajo. Sin éste el hombre pierde su visión, su confianza y la resolución de lograr sus metas.

૭૦૦ૐ

Le dénominateur commun de la réussite est le travail. Sans le travail, on perd la vision, la confiance et la détermination nécessaires pour réussir.

PAUL J. MEYER (b. 1928)

American Entrepreneur & Educator
Founder of The Success Motivation Institute's Companies
Empresario & Educador Americano
Fundador de las Empresas Success Motivation Institute
Homme d'affaires et éducateur américain
Fondateur des Entreprises Success Motivation Institute

July 21
21 de julio
21 juillet

There's one thing a business can't economize on: its reputation.

છાલ્જ

Si hay algo sobre lo cual ningún negocio puede economizar es su reputación.

છાલ્જ

S'il y a quelque chose sur laquelle aucune compagnie ne peut économiser, c'est sa réputation.

BETTER BUSINESS BUREAU

New York Times Advertising
Publicidad en el *New York Times*
Publicité parue dans le *New York Times*

He who every morning plans the activities of the day and follows that plan will find his way through the labyrinth of the busiest life. But when no plan is laid . . . chaos soon reigns.

&)(&

El que cada mañana planea las actividades del día y sigue su plan llevará el hilo que lo conducirá a través del laberinto de la vida más atareada. Sin embargo, si no establece un plan, pronto reinará el caos.

&)(&

Celui qui chaque matin planifie les activités de la journée et en suit le plan trouvera le fil qui le conduira à travers le labyrinthe de la vie la plus laborieuse. Cependant, si un plan n'est pas établi, bien vite régnera le chaos.

VICTOR HUGO (1802-1885)

French Writer
Escritor Francés
Écrivain français

Just because you can't see how to get to someplace doesn't mean you don't set the goal.

⊗⊗

El hecho de no poder ver cómo llegar a algún lugar no significa que no se debe fijar la meta.

⊗⊗

Le fait de ne pas voir comment atteindre un but ne veut pas dire que vous devez l'éliminer.

LLOYD DAVID WARD (b. 1949)

CEO Maytag
Ejecutivo Principal de la Compañía Maytag
PDG des Entreprises Maytag

I never remember feeling tired by work, though idleness exhausts me completely.

❧☙

No recuerdo haberme sentido cansado por el trabajo; sin embargo, la ociosidad me cansa completamente.

❧☙

Le travail ne me fatigue jamais, cependant l'oisiveté m'épuise.

ARTHUR CONAN DOYLE (1859-1930)

English Novelist
Novelista Inglés
Romancier anglais

July 25
25 de julio
25 juillet

Be anxious for nothing, but in everything in prayer and supplication, with thanksgiving, let your request be made known to God; and the peace of God, which surpasses all understanding, will guard your hearts and minds through Christ Jesus.

೫೦೦ಛ

No se inquieten por nada. En cualquier circunstancia recurran a la oración y a la súplica, junto a la acción de gracias, para presentar su petición a Dios. Entonces la paz de Dios, que es mucho mayor de lo que se puede imaginar, les guardará su corazón y sus pensamientos en Cristo Jesús.

೫೦೦ಛ

Ne vous inquiétez de rien; mais en toutes choses faites connaître vos besoins à Dieu par des prières et des supplications, avec des actions de grâce. Et la paix de Dieu, qui surpasse toute intelligence, gardera vos coeurs et vos pensées en Jésus-Christ.

THE BIBLE — LA BIBLIA — LA BIBLE

Philippians 4:6-7
Filipenses 4:6-7
Philippiens 4: 6-7

All that is necessary for the triumph of evil is for good men to do nothing.

જીલ્

El triunfo del mal depende de la apatía de la gente de bien.

જીલ્

La victoire du mal dépend de l'apathie des gens de bien.

EDMUND BURKE (1729-1797)

British Statesman & Writer
Hombre de Estado & Escritor Británico
Homme d'État et écrivain britannique

July 27
27 de julio
27 juillet

Of all people you will know in a lifetime, you are the only one you will never leave or lose. To the question of your life, you are the only answer. To the problems of your life, you are the only solution.

∞♥

De toda la gente que conocerás en el curso de su vida, tú eres la única que nunca podrás abandonar o perder. Eres la única respuesta a la pregunta de tu vida. Eres la única solución a los problemas de tu existencia.

∞♥

De tous ceux que vous allez connaître au cours de l'existence, vous êtes le seul que vous n'allez jamais quitter ou perdre. Vous êtes la seule réponse à la question sur votre raison de vivre. Vous êtes la seule solution aux problèmes de votre vie.

ANONYMOUS

Quoted in the "Dynamics of Personal Leadership"
Program by Paul J. Meyer
Founder of the Success Motivation Institute's Companies
Cita del Programa "Dinámica del Liderazgo Personal"
por Paul J. Meyer,
Fundador de Success Motivation International
Citation tirée du Programme
"Dynamique du Ledearship Personnel"
par Paul J. Meyer
Fondateur des entreprises Success Motivation International

Give some of your time to your fellow men. Even something small, always do something for others, something that will give you no other reward than the privilege of having done it.

༺༻

Hay que dar un poco de su tiempo al prójimo. Aunque sea poquito, siempre hay que hacer algo para los demás, algo que no le dará ningún otro beneficio que el privilegio de haberlo hecho.

༺༻

Il faut donner un peu de son temps à son prochain. Même si c'est peu, faites quelque chose pour autrui—quelque chose qui ne vous rapportera rien de plus que le privilège de l'avoir fait.

ALBERT SCHWEITZER (1875-1965)

Franco-German Philosopher, Musicologist & Physician
Filósofo, Musicólogo & Médico Franco-Alemán
Philosophe, musicologue et médecin franco-alleman

July 29
29 de julio
29 juillet

Beauty is an unexhausted source of joy for the one who knows how to find it.

৪৩৬৪

La belleza es una fuente inagotable de alegría para el que sabe como descubrirla.

৪৩৬৪

La beauté est une source inépuisable de joie pour celui qui sait la découvrir.

ALEXIS CARREL (1878-1944)

French Surgeon & Biologist, Author of *Man, This Unknown*
Cirujano & Biológo Francés, Autor de *El Hombre, Este Desconocido*
Chirurgien et biologiste français, auteur de *L'Homme, Cet Inconnu*

Politics are almost as exciting as war and quite as dangerous. In war you can only be killed once, but in politics many times.

୫୬ଔ

La política es casi tan excitante como la guerra y también casi tan peligrosa. En la guerra lo pueden matar una sola vez, pero en la política, muchas veces.

୫୬ଔ

La politique est presque aussi exaltante que la guerre, et presque aussi dangereuse. Dans la guerre, on ne peut être tué qu'une fois, mais dans une carrière politique, on peut l'être plusieurs fois.

WINSTON CHURCHILL (1874-1965)

British Politician & Prime Minister
Hombre de Estado & Primer Ministro Británico
Homme d'État et Premier Ministre britannique

July 31
31 de julio
31 juillet

We are all tattooed in our cradles with the beliefs of our tribes; the record may seem superficial, but is indelible.

❧☙

Desde la cuna, todos tenemos unos tatuajes de las creencias de nuestra tribu; puede que sean superficiales, pero son indelebles.

❧☙

Nous portons tous à la naissance les tatouages des croyances de notre tribu; ils peuvent être superficiels mais ils sont indélébiles.

OLIVER WENDELL HOLMES (1809-1894)

American Writer
Escritor Americano
Écrivain américain

AUGUST — AGOSTO — AOÛT

1 . . . . .ETHEL RÍOS DE BETANCOURT
2 . . . . .JOHN D. ROCKEFELLER
3 . . . . .DON PABLO CASALS

4 . . . . .EDOUARD F. LAFONTANT
5 . . . . .JOSEPH CONRAD
6 . . . . .VICTOR HUGO

7 . . . . .NIKOS KAZANTZAKIS
8 . . . . .FRANZ ERNST NEUMANN
9 . . . . .CHARLES DICKENS

10 . . . . .ANONYMOUS
11 . . . . .EMILIE BARNES
12 . . . . .JOHANN WOLFGANG VON GOETHE

13 . . . . .PREMIER CRUISE LINES ADVERTISING
14 . . . . .JOHN M. CAPOZZI
15 . . . . .GRAHAM GREENE

16 . . . . .GALILEO GALILEI
17 . . . . .WILLIAM HALE WHITE
 .(MARK RUTHERFORD)
18 . . . . .CHARLES DE GAULLE

19 . . . . .JACQUES MARITAIN
20 . . . . .THE BIBLE
21 . . . . .MARCUS AURELIUS ANTONINUS

22 . . . . .ANDRÉ GIDE
23 . . . . .LUIS A. FERRÉ
24 . . . . .ARAB PROVERB

25 . . . . .TAHAR BEN JELLOUN
26 . . . . .LUCIUS ANNAEUS SENECA
27 . . . . .PEDRO ALBIZU CAMPOS

28 . . . . .PAUL J. MEYER
29 . . . . .NORDOHL GREIG
30 . . . . .THEODORE ROOSEVELT
31 . . . . .JAIME BENÍTEZ

August 1
1 de agosto
1ᵉʳ août

When people come to you, don't be arrogant. Listen.

୫୦ଓଷ

Cuando alguien viene a usted, no sea arrogante. Escuche.

୫୦ଓଷ

Quand quelqu'un s'adresse à vous, ne soyez pas arrogant. Ecoutez-le.

ETHEL RÍOS DE BETANCOURT

Puerto Rican Educator
Educadora Puertorriqueña
Éducatrice portoricaine

August 2
2 de agosto
2 août

The ability to relate with other people is the most important. I will pay more for this ability than for any other thing under the sun.

ഓരു

La habilidad para relacionarse con la gente es lo más importante. Pagaré más por esta habilidad que por cualquier otra bajo el sol.

ഓരു

Le don d'établir de bons rapports avec les autres est d'une grande importance. Je payerais plus pour ce don que pour n'importe quel autre sous le soleil.

JOHN D. ROCKEFELLER (1839-1937)

American Entrepreneur
Industrial Americano
Industriel américain

August 3
3 de agosto
3 août

Every day I am born again. Every day a new phase of my life begins.

ॐ☯

Cada día nazco de nuevo; cada día empieza una nueva época de mi vida.

ॐ☯

Chaque jour je renais. Chaque jour une nouvelle phase de ma vie démarre.

DON PABLO CASALS (1878-1973)

Spanish Musician & Composer
Músico & Compositor Español
Musicien et compositeur espagnol

To the question of Sancho Panza: "Why are the dogs barking?" Don Quixote answered: "Because we are galloping." Your life should have a purpose so that you can say with your last breath: "I did not live in vain."

⬧⬥⬧

A la pregunta de Sancho Panza: "¿Por qué ladran los perros?" Don Quijote contestó: "Porque estamos cabalgando". Tu vida debe tener sentido para que puedas decir en tu último suspiro: "No he vivido en vano".

⬧⬥⬧

A la question de Sancho Panza: "Pourquoi les chiens aboient?" Don Quichotte répondit: "Parce que nous galopons". Donnez un sens à votre vie pour que vous puissiez dire dans votre dernier soupir: "Je n'ai pas vécu en vain".

EDOUARD F. LAFONTANT (b. 1932)

Master Motivator
Maestro Motivador
Maître motivateur

August 5
5 de agosto
5 août

Your mind is everything because everything is in your mind: the past and the future.

℀℀

El cerebro es todo porque todo está en el cerebro: el pasado y el futuro.

℀℀

Le cerveau est tout parce que tout est dans le cerveau: le passé et le futur.

JOSEPH CONRAD (1857-1924)

British Novelist
Novelista Británico
Romancier britannique

You can resist the invasion of an army, but not an idea.

༄༅

Se puede resistir la invasión de un ejército, pero no se puede resistir una idea.

༄༅

On peut résister à l'invasion d'une armée, mais pas à une idée.

VICTOR HUGO (1802-1885)

French Writer
Escritor Francés
Écrivain français

If we passionately believe in something that does not exist, we can create it. If something does not exist, it is because we have not desired it with enough passion.

ಸಂಗ

Si creemos apasionadamente en algo que no existe, podemos crearlo. Lo que no existe es porque no lo hemos deseado con suficiente pasión.

ಸಂಗ

Si nous croyons avec passion en quelque chose qui n'existe pas, nous pouvons la créer. Si quelque chose n'existe pas, c'est parce que nous ne l'avons pas désiré avec suffisamment de passion.

NIKOS KAZANTZAKIS (1883-1957)

Greek Writer, Author of *Zorba, The Greek*
Escritor Griego, Autor de *Zorba, el Greco*
Écrivain Grec, auteur de *Zorba, le Grec*

The greatest composer does not sit down to work because he feels inspired; he is inspired because he is working.

৪০৫৪

El gran compositor no se sienta a trabajar porque está inspirado, sino que se inspira porque está trabajando.

৪০৫৪

Le grand compositeur ne se met pas à travailler parce qu'il est inspiré; l'inspiration vient parce qu'il travaille.

FRANZ ERNST NEUMANN (1798-1895)

German Physicist
Físico Alemán
Physicien allemande

August 9
9 de agosto
9 août

Where's the good of putting things off? Strike while the iron is hot.

෨෬

¿Qué hay de bueno en posponer las cosas? Hay que forjar el hierro mientras esté rojo.

෨෬

Quel bénéfice peut on tirer à renvoyer les choses? Il faut battre le fer quand il est chaud.

CHARLES DICKENS (1812-1870)

English Novelist
Novelista Inglés
Romancier anglais

Nothing in the world can supersede persistence. Talent? Nothing is more common than unsuccessful men with talent. Genius? Ignored geniuses are almost a proverb. Education alone will not; the world is full of educated derelicts. Only determination and persistence are omnipotent.

ಬಂದಡ

Nada en el mundo sustituye a la persistencia. ¿Será el talento? No hay nada más común que ver a personas fracasadas con talento. ¿Será el Genio? Es casi proverbial ver genios no reconocidos. Ya se sabe que por sí sola la educación no es la respuesta porque el mundo está lleno de lunáticos muy educados. Solamente la determinación y la persistencia son omnipotentes.

ಬಂದಡ

Rien ne peut remplacer la persistance. Serait-ce le talent? Il n'y a rien de plus courant que les gens pleins de talents qui ont échoué. Serait-ce le génie? Les génies méconnus, c'est proverbial! L'éducation seule n'est pas non plus la réponse, parce que le monde est plein de parias très instruits. Seules la détermination et la persistance sont omnipotentes.

ANONYMOUS
ANONIMO
ANONYME

August 11
11 de agosto
11 août

Don't pile it, file it.

&ᘉᘂ&

No lo amontone, archívelo.

&ᘉᘂ&

N'empilez pas vos papiers, classez-les.

EMILIE BARNES

Author of *Timeless Treasures*
Autor de *Timeless Treasures*
Auteure du *Timeless Treasures*

August 12
12 de agosto
12 août

The fool and the wise are equally harmless, it is the half-wise and the half-foolish who must be feared the most.

୫୦୯୫

El loco y el sabio son igualmente inofensivos. A los que tenemos que temer es a los medio-locos y a los medio-sabios.

୫୦୯୫

Le fou et le sage sont également inoffensifs. Ce sont les demi-fous et les demi-sages que l'on doit craindre le plus.

JOHANN WOLFGANG VON GOETHE (1749-1832)

German Writer
Escritor Alemán
Écrivain allemand

August 13
13 de agosto
13 août

There is a tiny region in your brain reserved for memories; use the space wisely.

೪ೕಚಚ

Hay en su cerebro un pequeño espacio reservado a los recuerdos; use este espacio sabiamente.

೪ೕಚಚ

Il y a dans votre cerveau un petit espace réservé aux souvenirs; utilisez-le avec sagesse.

Don't hold a $1,000 meeting to solve a $100 problem.

೪ಾ೮ಙ

No celebre una reunión de $1,000 para resolver un problema de $100.

೪ಾ೮ಙ

N'organisez pas une réunion qui coûtera $1,000 pour résoudre un problème de $100.

JOHN M. CAPOZZI

American Airlines Executive
Un Dirigente de la American Airlines
Un dirigeant de la American Airlines

One must love every soul as if it were one's own child.

୫୬ୠ

Hay que amar a todas las almas como si cada una fuera su propio hijo.

୫୬ୠ

Il faut aimer toutes les âmes comme si chacune était celle de son propre enfant.

GRAHAM GREENE (b. 1904)

English Writer
Escritor Inglés
Écrivain anglais

You cannot really teach something to someone; you can only help him discover his own potential.

ഒരൂ

No se puede enseñar nada al hombre, sólo se le puede ayudar a descubrir lo que hay dentro de él.

ഒരൂ

En fait, on ne peut rien enseigner à l'homme, on peut seulement l'aider à découvrir sa propre valeur.

GALILEO GALILEI (1564-1642)

Italian Mathematician, Astronomer & Physicist
Matemático, astrónomo y físico italiano
Mathématicien, astronome et physicien italien

August 17
17 de agosto
17 aôut

I am not afraid of the future because I know yesterday and I love today.

ഇറ്റ

No temo el mañana porque conozco el ayer y me gusta el hoy.

ഇറ്റ

Je ne crains pas le futur parce que je connais le passé et j'aime le présent.

WILLIAM HALE WHITE (MARK RUTHERFORD) (1831-1913)

British Writer
Escritor Británico
Écrivain britannique

Glory is conquered only by those who always dream of it.

შავ

La gloria se entrega solamente a los que siempre han soñado con ella.

შავ

Pour conquérir la gloire, il faut sans cesse en rêver.

CHARLES DE GAULLE (1890-1970)

French General, Writer & Statesman
General, Escritor & Hombre de Estado Francés
Soldat, écrivain, Homme d'État français

Christianity taught men that love is worth more than intelligence.

৩৩০৪

El cristianismo ha enseñado a los hombres que el amor vale más que la inteligencia.

৩৩০৪

Le christianisme a enseigné aux hommes que l'amour vaut plus que l'intelligence.

JACQUES MARITAIN (1882-1973)

French Philosopher
Filósofo Francés
Philosophe français

. . . If you have faith the size of a mustard seed, you will say to this mountain, 'Move from here to there,' and it will move; and nothing will be impossible for you.

ઇઉભ

. . . Si tuvieran fe como un granito de moztaza, le dirían a este cerro, quítate de ahí y pónte más allá, y el cerro obedecerá. Nada les sería imposible.

ઇઉભ

. . . Si vous avez une foi aussi minime qu'un grain de sénevé, vous direz à cette montagne: Déplace-toi et elle se déplacera; et rien ne vous sera impossible.

THE BIBLE—LA BIBLIA—LA BIBLE

St. Matthew 17:20
San Mateo 17:20
St. Matthieu 17:20

August 21
21 de agosto
21 août

When you get up in the morning, remember how precious is the privilege to be alive, to breathe, to be happy.

৪০৫৪

Al levantarte por la mañana, recuerda cuán precioso es el privilegio de vivir, de respirar, de ser feliz.

৪০৫৪

En te levant le matin, rappelle-toi combien précieux est le privilège de vivre, de respirer, d'être heureux.

MARCUS AURELIUS ANTONINUS (121-180)

Roman Emperor & Philosopher
Emperador & Filósofo Romano
Empereur et philosophe romain

To envy the happiness of others is folly; one could not use it. There is no standard type of happiness, it is individually tailor made.

৪১০৪৪

Envidiar la felicidad de los demás es una locura; no se podría disfrutar de ella. La felicidad no se consigue en serie sino a la medida.

৪১০৪৪

Envier le bonheur d'autrui, c'est folie; on ne saurait pas s'en servir. Le bonheur ne se veut pas tout fait, mais sur mesure.

ANDRÉ GIDE (1869-1951)

French Writer
Escritor Francés
Écrivain françois

August 23
23 de agosto
23 août

The challenge is not to let the sons of today's poverty become the fathers of tomorrow's poverty any longer.

›‹

El reto es no permitir por más tiempo que los hijos de la pobreza de hoy se conviertan en los padres de la pobreza en el mañana.

›‹

Le défi est de ne pas permettre plus longtemps que les enfants de la pauvreté d'aujourdhui deviennent les pères de la pauvreté de demain.

LUIS A. FERRÉ (1904-2003)

Former Governor of Puerto Rico
Ex Gobernador de Puerto Rico
Ex-gouverneur de Porto Rico

The true mosque is the one built at the bottom of the soul.

৪০৫৪

La verdadera mezquita es la que está construida en el fondo del alma.

৪০৫৪

La véritable mosquée est celle qui est construite au fond de l'âme.

ARAB PROVERB
PROVERBIO ARABE
PROVERBE ARABE

In my country
We do not lend
We share.

&⊃☾⊰

En nuestro país
No se presta
Se comparte.

&⊃☾⊰

Dans mon pays
On ne prête pas
On partage.

TAHAR BEN JELLOUN (b. 1944)

Moroccan Writer
Escritor Marroquí
Écrivain marocain

All my wealth is within myself.

୫୬୯ୟ

Todos mis bienes están en mí.

୫୬୯ୟ

Toutes mes richesses sont en moi.

LUCIUS ANNAEUS SENECA (c. 4 B.C.-c. 65 A.D.)

Roman Philosopher
Filósofo Romano
Philosophe romain

He who is not proud of his origin will never be worth much because he downgrades his own self-esteem.

୫୦୯ଓ

Aquel que no está orgulloso de su origen no valdrá nunca nada, porque empieza por despreciarse a sí mismo.

୫୦୯ଓ

Celui qui n'est pas fier de son origine ne vaudra jamais rien parce qu'il sous-estime sa propre personne.

PEDRO ALBIZU CAMPOS (1891-1965)

Puerto Rican Patriot
Patriota Puertorriqueño
Patriote portoricain

August 28
28 de agosto
28 août

The most successful leaders are those who recognize the creative potential of every person on their team and make productive use of it.

&&

Los líderes de mayor éxito son aquellos que reconocen el potencial creativo de cada una de las personas que trabajan con ellos y lo utilizan productivamente.

&&

Les leaders qui atteignent les plus hauts niveaux de réussite sont ceux qui peuvent évaluer le potentiel de créativité de chaque membre de son équipe et en tirer profit.

PAUL J. MEYER (b. 1928)

American Entrepreneur & Educator
Founder of The Success Motivation Institute's Companies
Empresario & Educador Americano
Fundador de las Empresas Success Motivation Institute
Homme d'affaires et educateur américain
Fundateur des entreprises Success Motivation Institute

August 29
29 de agosto
29 août

We cannot consider peace as one of our tangible possesions. We have to conquer it every day.

୧୦୧୨

La paz no se puede considerar como un objeto que poseemos. Hay que conquistarla siempre.

୧୦୧୨

La paix n'est pas comparable à un objet précieux qui nous appartient. Il faut toujours la conquérir.

NORDOHL GREIG (1902-1943)

Norwegian Writer
Escritor Noruego
Écrivain norvégien

The credit belongs to the man who is actually in the arena, whose face is marred by dust and sweat and blood, who strives valiantly, who errs and comes up short again and again; because there is no effort without error and shortcomings; who knows the great devotion, who spends himself in a worthy cause, who at best knows in the end the high achievement of triumph and who at worst, if he fails while daring greatly, knows his place shall never be with those timid and cold souls who know neither victory nor defeat.

℘ℂ℘

El mérito pertenece al hombre que está en el ruedo; cuyo rostro está empañado por el polvo y por el sudor y la sangre; que lucha valientemente, que yerra y se queda corto una y otra vez; que conoce de los grandes entusiasmos, de las grandes devociones, del vivir momento a momento y gasta sus energías por una causa digna; que en su mejor hora, saborea al final el triunfo del propósito noble; y que en su peor hora, si fracasa, al menos cae tras un gran despliegue de audacia, paciencia y pensamiento por lo que su sitial nunca estará junto a aquellos seres fríos y tímidos que jamás han probado ni el triunfo ni la derrota.

℘ℂ℘

L'honneur revient à celui qui est descendu dans l'arène et dont le visage est couvert de sueur, de poussière et de sang; à celui qui a lutté vaillamment, à celui qui s'est trompé et a persévéré malgré ses erreurs car il n'y a pas d'action sans embûches et sans erreurs; à celui qui se dévoue corps et âme pour une cause valable sachant que la gloire l'attend s'il gagne, ou s'il échoue, qu'au moins il échoue en osant de grandes choses de sorte que sa place ne soit jamais parmi ces âmes froides et timides qui ne connaissent ni la victoire ni la défaite.

THEODORE ROOSEVELT (1858-1919)

26th President of the United States of America
26° Presidente de los Estados Unidos de América
26e Président des Etats-Unis d'Amérique

The real profession to which all the others must relate, and without which they are worthless, is the profession of being HUMAN BEINGS. People ready to learn, to create, to be generous with their fellow men and demanding with themselves.

֍

La verdadera profesión a la cual todas las demás deben redimirse y sin la cual ninguna de las demás vale gran cosa, es la profesión de ser SERES HUMANOS: Gente en disponibilidad para aprender, para crear, para ser generoso con el semejante y exigente consigo mismo.

֍

La vraie profession que toutes les autres doivent inclure et sans laquelle elles ne valent pas grand' chose est celle de demeurer des ETRES HUMAINS toujours prêts à apprendre, à créer, à être généreux envers ses semblables et exigeants avec eux mêmes.

JAIME BENÍTEZ (1908-2001)

Dean & President of the University of Puerto Rico
Rector & Presidente de la Universidad de Puerto Rico
Recteur et président de l'Université de Porto Rico

SEPTEMBER — SEPTIEMBRE — SEPTEMBRE

1 . . . . FRANÇOIS MARIE AROUET — dit
VOLTAIRE
2 . . . . EDOUARD F. LAFONTANT
3 . . . . ARTHUR SCHOPENHAUER

4 . . . . PAUL J. MEYER
5 . . . . GEORG CHRISTOPH LICHTENBERG
6 . . . . JOHNATHAN SWIFT

7 . . . . SATCHEL PAIGE
8 . . . . LUIS A. FERRÉ
9 . . . . MOCHARRAFODDIN SAADI

10 . . . . ANONYMOUS
11 . . . . CHINESE PROVERB
12 . . . . MARTIN HABERMAN

13 . . . . LUCILLE BALL
14 . . . . LUCIUS ANNAEUS SENECA
15 . . . . THE BIBLE

16 . . . . MIGUEL DE UNAMUNO
17 . . . . KAROL WOJTYLA, POPE JOHN PAUL II
18 . . . . CONFUCIUS

19 . . . . LAO-TZU
20 . . . . JOHANN WOLFGANG VON
GOETHE
21 . . . . MAKSIMOVITCH GORKI

22 . . . . PERICLES
23 . . . . TOMMY LASORDA
24 . . . . JAMES ALLEN

25 . . . . PAUL-ÉMILE VICTOR
26 . . . . GEORGE S. PATTON
27 . . . . QUINTUS HORATIUS FLACCUS

28 . . . . DAVID BAIRD
29 . . . . HISDAI IBN SHAPRUT
30 . . . . KOFI ANNAN

September 1
1 de septiembre
1er septembre

Your work should be a challenge, not a burden; a blessing, not a bore.

⁂❧

Su trabajo debe ser un reto, no una carga; una bendición, no un aburrimiento.

⁂❧

Votre travail doit être un défi et non un fardeau; une bénédiction et non un ennui.

FRANçOIS MARIE AROUET — dit VOLTAIRE (1694-1778)

French Writer
Escritor Francés
Écrivain français

According to Robert Reich, former Secretary of Labor and a professor at Harvard University, the surest path to profitability and productivity is the treatment of every employee as an asset to be developed and not as a cost to be cut. The success of any organization depends on the application of this principle, an exciting factor of progress in today's enterprises which has touched a sensitive cord in the mind and heart of many CEO's and other decision makers at the dawn of this New Millennium.

ಸಂಗ

Según Robert Reich, pasado Secretario del Trabajo y Profesor en la Universidad de Harvard, el camino más seguro hacia las ganancias y la productividad es de tratar cada empleado como un activo a desarrollar y no como unos costos a eliminar. El éxito de cada organización depende de la aplicación de esta indudable verdad, que es uno de los factores más estimulantes del progreso de las empresas modernas. Este pensamiento ha tocado unas fibras sensitivas en la mente y el corazón de muchos dirigentes y otros líderes en el umbral del Nuevo Milenio.

ಸಂಗ

Selon Robert Reich, ancien Secrétaire du Travail et Professeur à l'Université Harvard, la voie la plus sûre vers la rentabilité et la productivité consiste à traiter chaque employé comme un actif à développer et non comme une dépense à éliminer. Le succès de toute organisation va de pair avec l'application de ce principe qui constitue un facteur très important de progrès dans une entreprise moderne et qui heureusement a touché une corde sensible dans l'esprit et le coeur de nombreux PDG et d'autres décideurs à l'aube de ce Nouveau Millénaire.

EDOUARD F. LAFONTANT (b. 1932)

Master Motivator
Maestro Motivador
Maître motivateur

No difference in rank, position, or birth, is so great as the gulf which separates the countless millions who use their head only in the service of their belly . . . and those very few and rare persons who have the courage to say: No! It is too good for that, my head shall be active in its own service; it shall try to comprehend the wondrous and varied spectacle of this world, and then reproduce it in some form, whether as art or as literature, that may answer to his character as an individual.

෩෨

Ninguna diferencia de rango, de posición o de origen social es tan profunda como la brecha que separa los que consagran su inteligencia únicamente al servicio de su barriga y las muy escasas personas que tienen la valentía de decir: No, mi cerebro es un instrumento demasiado bello para usarlo sólo para ese propósito. Debo consagrarlo exclusivamente a su propio servicio: el de tratar de comprender el espectáculo maravilloso y variado del universo y convertirlo en una obra de arte o de literatura digna de su propia personalidad.

෩෨

Aucune différence de rang, de position ou d'origine sociale n'est aussi profonde que le fossé qui sépare ceux qui consacrent leur intelligence uniquement au service de leur ventre et les très rares personnes qui ont le courage de dire: Non, mon cerveau est un trop bel instrument pour un pareil usage, mon cerveau doit être consacré exclusivement à son propre rôle. Il doit essayer de comprendre le spectacle merveilleux et varié de l'univers et le convertir en une oeuvre d'art ou de littérature qui reflète sa personnalité.

ARTHUR SCHOPENHAEUR (1788-1860)

German Philosopher, *On Genius*
Filósofo Alemán, *On Genius*
Philosophe allemand, *On Genius*

It is through their work that most people write the story of their lives. They are both author and principal character. They are free to be the hero or the villain . . . to succeed or to fail.

೮೦೮೮

Es por medio de su trabajo que la mayoría de los hombres escriben la historia de sus vidas. Ellos son al mismo tiempo los autores y los personajes principales. Tienen la libertad de ser los héroes o los villanos . . . lograr el éxito o el fracaso.

೮೦೮೮

C'est par leur travail que la majorité des hommes écrivent l'histoire de leur vie. Ils sont à la fois les auteurs et les personnages principaux. Ils ont la liberté d'être ou les héros ou les vilains . . . de réussir ou d'échouer.

PAUL J. MEYER (b. 1928)

American Entrepreneur & Educator
Founder of The Success Motivation Institute's Companies
Empresario & Educador Americano
Fundador de las Empresas Success Motivation Institute
Homme d'affaires et éducateur américain
Fondateur des entreprises Success Motivation Institute

Everyone is a genius at least once a year.

৪০৫৪

Somos geniales por lo menos una vez al año.

৪০৫৪

Nous sommes tous des génies au moins une fois l'an.

GEORG CHRISTOPH LICHTENBERG (1742-1799)

German Philosopher, Physicist, Satirist & Humorist
Filósofo, Físico, Satírico & Humorista Alemán
Philosophe, physicien, satiriste et humoriste allemand

Vision is the art of seeing things invisible.

ഇറ്റ

Visión es el arte de ver lo invisible.

ഇറ്റ

La vision est l'art de voir l'invisible.

JOHNATHAN SWIFT (1667-1745)

English Writer
Escritor Inglés
Écrivain anglais

Nobody can avoid being born ordinary, but nobody should stay common.

ଔେଓ

Ningún hombre puede evitar haber nacido ordinario, pero ninguno tiene que ser común.

ଔେଓ

Personne ne peut éviter de naître médiocre, mais personne ne devrait rester médiocre.

SATCHEL PAIGE (1906-1982)
or Leroy Robert Paige

American Baseball Athlete
Beisbolero Americano
Joueur américain de baseball

September 8
8 de septiembre
8 septembre

Patriotism is neither the flag, neither the national anthem nor the noisy marches. It's creative effort, the sense of social responsibility, the respect for the law and the love of freedom.

଼ଠଓଷ

La Patria no es bandera ni es himno, ni es ruido. La Patria es esfuerzo creador, es sentido de responsabilidad social, es respeto a la razón y es amor a la libertad.

଼ଠଓଷ

La Patrie n'est ni le drapeau, ni l'hymne national, ni les manifestations bruyantes. C'est l'effort créateur, le sens des responsabilités sociales, le respect de la loi et l'amour de la liberté.

LUIS A. FERRÉ (1904-2003)

Former Governor of Puerto Rico
Ex Gobernador de Puerto Rico
Ex-gouverneur de Porto Rico

297

September 9
9 de septiembre
9 septembre

Before you win with the sword, try to win with persuasion.

ಬಂಡ

Antes de vencer con la espada, procura vencer con la persuasión.

ಬಂಡ

Avant de vaincre avec l'épée, essayez de vaincre avec la persuasion.

MOCHARRAFODDIN SAADI (1213-1292)

Persian Poet
Poeta Persa
Poète perse

298

Being human is very simple and very difficult at the same time. It consists of being intelligent enough to ignore the foolishness of others and good enough to forgive their wickedness.

കൗരു

Ser humano es muy sencillo y muy difícil a la vez. Consiste en saber ser tan inteligente que se disimule la tontería de los demás y en saber ser tan bueno que se perdone la maldad ajena.

കൗരു

Etre humain est à la fois très simple et très difficile. Cela consiste à être assez intelligent pour ignorer les sottises des autres et assez bon pour pardonner leur méchanceté.

ANONYMOUS
ANONIMO
ANONYME

September 11
11 de septiembre
11 septembre

Always direct your face toward the sun, thus the shadows will always stay behind you.

಄೦ೲ

Dirige siempre tu rostro hacia el sol, entonces las sombras quedarán siempre atrás.

಄೦ೲ

Oriente toujours ton visage vers le soleil, ainsi les ombres resteront toujours derrière toi.

CHINESE PROVERB
PROVERBIO CHINO
PROVERBE CHINOIS

Before we can go on making workers, we must first make people.

❧❧

Antes de poder adiestrar al trabajador, tenemos primero que preparar al hombre.

❧❧

Avant de former des travailleurs, nous devons d'abord former des êtres humains.

MARTIN HABERMAN

September 13
13 de septiembre
13 septembre

The secret to staying young is to be honest, to eat slowly and to lie about your age.

₧℃

El secreto para mantenerse joven es ser honesto, comer lentamente y mentir sobre su edad.

₧℃

Le secret pour garder sa jeunesse consiste à être honnête, à manger lentement et à cacher son âge.

LUCILLE BALL (1911-1989)

American Comedian
Comediante Americana
Comédienne américaine

Everybody is a divinity in disguise, from time to time we have a flash of pure intelligence; the rest of the time we are playing the fool.

ಬಂ಄ಚ

Todo individuo es una divinidad disfrazada. De vez en cuando, tenemos un relámpago de pura inteligencia; el resto del tiempo somos unos loquitos.

ಬಂ಄ಚ

Tout individu est une divinité masquée. De temps en temps nous avons un éclair de pure intelligence; le reste du temps, nous faisons des sottises.

LUCIUS ANNAEUS SENECA (c. 4 B.C.-c. 65 A.D.)

Roman Philosopher
Filósofo Romano
Philosophe romain

September 15
15 de septiembre
15 septembre

Let this mind be in you which was also in Christ Jesus.

೫೦೦೪

Tengan unos con otros las mismas disposiciones que tuvo Cristo Jesús.

೫೦೦೪

Ayez en vous les sentiments qui étaient en Jésus-Christ.

THE BIBLE — LA BIBLIA — LA BIBLE

Philippians 2:5
Filipenses 2:5
Philippéens 2:5

Happiness is something one lives and feels; it is not something to reason or to define.

ഇൠ

La felicidad es algo que se vive y se siente, y que no se razona ni se define.

ഇൠ

Le bonheur est une chose qui se vit et se sent, et non qui se raisonne et se définit.

MIGUEL DE UNAMUNO (1864-1936)

Spanish Writer
Escritor Español
Écrivain espagnol

It is on Love that the future depends.

ଶ୦ଓଃ

Es del Amor que depende el futuro.

ଶ୦ଓଃ

C'est de l'Amour que dépend l'avenir.

KAROL WOJTYLA (b. 1920)

Pope John Paul II
Papa Juan Pablo II
Pape Jean-Paul II

Choose a work that you like, and you will never have to work in your life.

ഇൗങ്ങ

Escoge un trabajo que ames y no tendrás que trabajar ni un solo día de tu vida.

ഇൗങ്ങ

Choisissez un travail que vous aimez et vous n'aurez pas à travailler un seul jour de votre vie.

CONFUCIUS (c. 551-479 B.C.)

Chinese Philosopher
Filósofo Chino
Philosophe chinois

September 19
19 de septiembre
19 septembre

Thanks to hazard, a man can reign over the world for some time. But with love and goodness, he can reign over the world forever.

୫୦ଔଓ

Gracias a un efecto del azar, un hombre puede dominar el mundo por algún tiempo. Pero, en virtud del amor y de la bondad, él puede reinar sobre el mundo para siempe.

୫୦ଔଓ

Grâce à un effet du hasard, un homme peut régner sur le monde pendant un certain temps. Mais, par la puissance de l'amour et de la bonté, il peut régner sur le monde à jamais.

LAO-TZU (500 B.C.)

Chinese Philosopher
Filósofo Chino
Philosophe chinois

Do you want to be happy? Travel with two bags: one for giving, the other one for receiving.

ঔ෩ঔ

¿Quieres vivir feliz? Viaja con dos sacos, uno para dar, otro para recibir.

ঔ෩ঔ

Veux-tu vivre heureux? Voyage avec deux sacs, un pour donner, l'autre pour recevoir.

JOHANN WOLFGANG VON GOETHE (1749-1832)

German Poet
Poeta Alemán
Poète allemand

September 21
21 de septiembre
21 septembre

When work is a pleasure, life is beautiful. But when it is a burden, life becomes slavery.

❧⟐

Cuando el trabajo es un placer, la vida es bella. Pero cuando nos es impuesto, la vida es una esclavitud.

❧⟐

Quand le travail est un plaisir, la vie est belle. Mais quand le travail devient une servitude la vie est minable.

MAKSIMOVITCH GORKI (1868-1936)

Russian Writer
Escritor Ruso
Écrivain russe

September 22
22 de septiembre
22 septembre

There is no happiness without freedom and no freedom without courage.

༄༅

No hay felicidad sin libertad, ni libertad sin valentía.

༄༅

Il n'est point de bonheur sans liberté, ni de liberté sans courage.

PERICLES (v. 495 – 429 B.C.)

Athenian Statesman
Hombre de Estado Ateniense
Homme d'État athénien

September 23
23 de septiembre
23 septembre

The difference between the impossible and the possible lies in a person's determination.

৪০৫

La diferencia entre imposible y posible se encuentra en su determinación.

৪০৫

La différence entre l'impossible et le possible se trouve dans votre détermination.

TOMMY LASORDA (b. 1927)

Baseball Manager — Los Angeles Dodgers
Director del Equipo de Beisbol Dodgers de los Angeles, California
Directeur d'équipe de baseball de Los Angeles, Californie

September 24
24 de septiembre
24 septembre

The universe does not favor the greedy, the dishonest, the vicious; although on the mere surface it may sometimes appear to do so; it helps the honest, the magnanimous, the virtuous.

༄༅

Parece que el mundo favorece a veces a los mezquinos, los deshonestos y los viciosos, es un error. El mundo alienta la honestidad, la generosidad y la ética.

༄༅

Apparemment, le monde favorise parfois les mesquins, les malhonnêtes et les vicieux. Erreur! Le monde encourage l'honnêteté, la générosité et le courage.

JAMES ALLEN (1864-1912)

English Writer, Author of the book *As a Man Thinketh*
Escritor Inglés, Autor del libro *As a Man Thinketh*
Écrivain anglais, auteur du livre *As a Man Thinketh*

September 25
25 de septiembre
25 septembre

Living is waking up in the middle of the night and feeling impatient to see a new day, it's to marvel that the daily miracle is made again for us, it's to have happy sleepless nights.

ഇറൽ

Vivir, es despertarse de noche con la impaciencia del día próximo, es maravillarse del milagro cotidiano que se reproduce una vez más para nosotros, es alegrarse de los insomnios.

ഇറൽ

Vivre, c'est se réveiller la nuit dans l'impatience du jour à venir, c'est s'émerveiller que le miracle quotidien se reproduise pour nous une fois encore, c'est avoir des insomnies de joie.

PAUL-ÉMILE VICTOR (b. 1907)

French Explorer
Explorador Francés
Explorateur français

I don't measure a man's success by how high he climbs but how high he bounces when he hits bottom.

ಬಿೆಯ

Yo no mido el éxito de una persona por la magnitud de sus victorias sino por su capacidad de alcanzar la cima del éxito después de haber tocado el fondo del abismo de la derrota.

ಬಿೆಯ

Je ne mesure pas la réussite d'un homme à sa position dans l'échelle sociale, mais à sa capacité de rebondir avec force lorsqu'il a touché le fond de l'abîme.

GEORGE S. PATTON (1885-1945)

United States of America Army General
General del Ejército de los Estados Unidos de América
Général de l'Armée des États-Unis d'Amérique

September 27
27 de septiembre
27 septembre

On the oceans, on the roads, we pursue happiness, but it is here, in ourselves!

෨෦෪

Perseguimos la felicidad sobre los océanos, sobre los grandes caminos, pero la felicidad está aquí, en nosotros.

෨෦෪

Sur les océans, sur les grands chemins, nous cherchons le bonheur. Mais il est ici en nous-mêmes, le bonheur.

QUINTUS HORATIUS FLACCUS (65-8 B.C.)

Latin Poet
Poeta Latino
Poète latin

See to it that the face you see in the mirror when you wake up is agreeable. Perhaps you will not see it again during the day but other people will.

ᎬᏉᏨ

Asegúrese que la cara que usted ve por la mañana en el espejo sea una agradable. Quizás usted no la verá más durante el día, pero otros sí la verán.

ᎬᏉᏨ

Faites en sorte que le visage que vous voyez le matin dans le miroir soit un visage agréable. Peut-être vous ne le verrez plus de la journée, mais d'autres le verront.

DAVID BAIRD

September 29
29 de septiembre
29 septembre

Your son at five is your master, at ten, your slave, at fifteen your double, and after that, your friend or your foe, it depends on how you raised him.

೮೦೮೮

A los cinco años, su hijo es su amo, a los diez años, es su esclavo, a los quince es su doble y después de eso, es su amigo o su enemigo, dependiendo de la educación que recibió de usted.

೮೦೮೮

A cinq ans, votre fils est votre maître, à dix ans il est votre esclave, à quinze ans il est votre copie; après, il est votre ami ou votre ennemi, cela dépend de votre façon de l'élever.

HISDAI IBN SHAPRUT (10th century A.D. — 915-975)

Jewish Scholar
Letrado Judio
Érudit juif

We cannot live in two worlds; there is only one world. We cannot live in a society where extreme wealth dwells next to extreme poverty and do nothing about it and hope it is going to work in the long run.

୫୬୪ଔ

No podemos vivir en dos mundos, sólo existe uno. No se puede vivir en una sociedad en la que conviven juntas la extrema riqueza y la extrema pobreza y no hacer nada al respecto y esperar que esto sea sustentable a la larga.

୫୬୪ଔ

Nous ne pouvons pas vivre dans deux mondes, il n'existe qu'un seul monde. On ne peut pas vivre dans une société où l'extrême richesse côtoie l'extrême pauvreté, ne rien faire et croire que cette situation peut durer indéfiniment.

KOFI ANNAN (b. 1938)

7th Secretary General of the United Nations (2002)
7° Secretario General de las Naciones Unidas (2002)
7e Secrétaire général des Nations Unies (2002)

OCTOBER – OCTUBRE – OCTOBRE

1 . . . . .JOHN DONNE
2 . . . . .EDOUARD F. LAFONTANT
                    FAVORITE PRAYER
3 . . . . .RABINDRANATH TAGORE

4 . . . . .THE TALMUD
5 . . . . .AN AMERICAN GLASSBLOWER
6 . . . . .ALEX MALDONADO

7 . . . . .MIGUEL DE CERVANTES
                    SAAVEDRA
8 . . . . .PAUL J. MEYER
9 . . . . .ADVERTISING BY NISSAN
                    MOTORS
10 . . . . .JOSEPH ADDISON
11 . . . . .ARAB PROVERB
12 . . . . .LUCIUS ANNAEUS SENECA

13 . . . . .JAMES ALLEN
14 . . . . .CHARLES DE GAULLE
15 . . . . .HAITIAN PROVERB

16 . . . . .BAIRD THOMAS SPALDING III
17 . . . . .ARTHUR SCHOPENHAUER
18 . . . . .ANONYMOUS

19 . . . . .ANDRÉ MAUROIS
20 . . . . .MARTIN LUTHER KING JR.
21 . . . . .JAPANESE PROVERB

22 . . . . .ABRAHAM LINCOLN
23 . . . . .FARID AL-DIN 'ATTAR
24 . . . . .ERNESTO RAMOS ANTONINI

25 . . . . .CHINESE PROVERB
26 . . . . .FRANK LLOYD WRIGHT
27 . . . . .JOSE C. DUARTE DA SILVEIRA

28 . . . . .ALBERT EINSTEIN
29 . . . . .LOUIS PASTEUR
30 . . . . .THE BIBLE
31 . . . . .PREMIER MALDONADO

October 1
1 de octubre
1er octobre

No man is an island entirely of itself. Every man is a piece of the continent, a part of the main . . . any man's death diminishes me, because I am involved in mankind, and therefore, never send to know for whom the bell tolls; it tolls for you.

୧୦୯୫

Ningún hombre es una isla en sí, cada hombre es una pieza del continente, una parte del todo . . . La muerte de cualquier hombre me disminuye porque estoy envuelto en la humanidad, así que nunca manda a preguntar por quien doblan las campanas; doblan por ti.

୧୦୯୫

Aucun homme n'est une île solitaire, chaque homme est un morceau du continent, une partie du tout . . . La mort de n'importe quel homme me diminue parce que je fais partie du genre humain. Aussi, ne cherche jamais à savoir pour qui sonne le glas, c'est pour toi qu'il sonne.

JOHN DONNE (1573-1631)

English Poet
Poeta Inglés
Poète anglais

Lord! I am not what I would like to be,
I am not what I could be,
I am not what I should be;
But thank you Lord
For not being what I was.

80C3

Señor! No soy lo que quisiera ser,
No soy lo que pudiera ser,
No soy lo que debería ser;
Pero gracias Señor
Por no ser lo que yo era.

80C3

Seigneur! Je ne suis pas ce que je voudrais être
Je ne suis pas ce que je pourrais être
Je ne suis pas ce que je devrais être
Mais, je vous remercie Seigneur
De ne pas être ce que j'étais.

EDOUARD F. LAFONTANT (b. 1932)

One of my favorite prayers
Una de mis oraciones favoritas
Une de mes prières préferées

October 3
3 de octubre
3 octobre

I slept and I dreamed that life was joy,
I awoke and I saw that life was service,
I served and I saw that by serving I found joy.

ಐಂಐ

Dormí y soñé que la vida era alegría,
Desperté y ví que la vida era servicio,
Serví y ví que en el servicio se encuentra la alegría.

ಐಂಐ

En dormant j'ai rêvé que la vie était joie,
A mon réveil j'ai vu que la vie était service,
J'ai servi et en servant, j'ai trouvé la joie.

RABINDRANATH TAGORE (1861-1941)

Indian Poet
Poeta Indio
Poète indien

Don't scorn any blessing, no matter from whom it comes.

ᘓᘔ

No menosprecie la bendición de ningún hombre.

ᘓᘔ

Ne dédaigne la bénédiction d'aucun homme.

THE TALMUD
EL TALMUD
LE TALMUD

I have never seen a color I did not like.

৯৩৫৪

Yo nunca he visto un color que no me ha gustado.

৯৩৫৪

Je n'ai jamais vu une couleur que je n'ai pas aimée.

AN AMERICAN GLASSBLOWER

Expression Heard on TV (CNN)
Expresión Escuchada por TV (CNN)
De un Soplador de Vidrio Americano
Expression entendue à la TV (CNN)
d'un souffleur de verre américain

During his eight years as mayor of New York, Rudolph Giuliani showed a different kind of "courage" — the political courage to fight against what he called "the anti-development philosophy — a strand, a very dangerous one, that opposes development of any kind, . . . any place." A city that does not develop, build and rebuild, create and recreate, will, as Giuliani put it, "just atrophy. It just dies."

സൂൽ

En sus ocho años como Alcalde [de Nueva York, Rudolph Giuliani] demostró otra clase de valentía, la valentía política de luchar en contra de lo que llama "La filosofía anti-desarrollo . . . un ramal, muy peligroso, que se opone a toda clase de desarrollo, . . . en cualquier lugar." Una ciudad, como todo lo que vive, que no se desarrolle, que no construya y reconstruya, que no crea y recrea, como dice Giuliani "sencillamente se atrofia. Sencillamente se muere."

സൂൽ

Au cours de ses huit ans à la Mairie de New York, Rudolph Giuliani a fait preuve d'une nouvelle forme de courage politique, celle de lutter contre ce qu'il appelle "la philosophie anti-développement . . ." une déviation très dangereuse qui s'oppose à tout développement, quelqu' en soit la forme et le secteur. Une ville qui ne se développe pas, qui ne construit pas, qui ne reconstruit pas, qui ne crée pas, qui ne recrée pas, comme dit Giuliani, "simplement s'atrophie. Simplement meurt."

ALEX MALDONADO

Puerto Rican Journalist, writing about Rudolph Giuliani,
Mayor of New York and Person of the Year 2001
Periodista Puertorriqueño, escribiendo acerca de Rudolph Giuliani,
Alcalde de Nueva York y Persona del Año 2001
Journaliste portoricain, écrivant sur Rudolph Giulini,
Maire de New York et personnalité de l'année 2001

October 7
7 de octubre
7 octobre

A tooth is worth more than a diamond.

༄༅

Un diente vale más que un diamante.

༄༅

Une dent vaut plus qu'un diamant.

MIGUEL DE CERVANTES SAAVEDRA (1547-1616)

Spanish Writer, Author of *Don Quixote*
Escritor Español, Autor de *Don Quijote*
Écrivain espagnol, auteur de *Don Quichotte*

If you stubbornly resist change, you will live but a single, uneventful life no matter how serene it may be. But if you welcome and accept change, you will live many lives . . . all equally rewarding.

෴

La persona que con terquedad se resiste al cambio, no vive más que una sola vida tediosa, sin importar lo tranquila que sea. Pero aquel que acoge los cambios con beneplácito y los acepta, vive muchas vidas, todas ellas igualmente satisfactorias.

෴

Celui qui obstinément résiste au changement ne vivra qu'une seule vie, sereine mais banale. Mais celui qui accueille avec joie et accepte le changement vivra plusieurs vies les unes aussi exaltantes que les autres.

PAUL J. MEYER (b. 1928)

American Entrepreneur & Educator
Founder of the Success Motivation Institute companies
Empresario & Educador Americano
Fundador de las Empresas Success Motivation Institute
Homme d'affaires et éducateur américain
Fondateur des entreprises Success Motivation Institute

October 9
9 de octubre
9 octobre

For everything in life, there is someone who turns it into something more than a product or a job or a service. He makes it a passion. And his creations seem to be imbued with a soul.

ೞೞೞ

En todas las cosas de la vida, aparece alguien que las transforma en algo más que un producto, un trabajo o un servicio. Las convierte en una pasión y parece que sus creaciones vibran con alma propia.

ೞೞೞ

Dans la vie on peut toujours trouver quelqu'un capable de transformer n'importe quoi en quelque chose de plus qu'un produit, une fonction, ou un service. Quelqu'un capable d'en faire une passion, quelqu'un dont toutes les créations semblent imprégnées d'une âme.

Nothing that can be acquired without work and effort has a true value.

৪৩৫

Nada que pueda conseguirse sin pena y sin trabajo, es verdaderamente valioso.

৪৩৫

Sans effort et sans travail, on ne peut rien acquérir de vraiment valable.

JOSEPH ADDISON (1672-1719)

English Essayist & Poet
Ensayista & Poeta Inglés
Essayiste et poète anglais

October 11
11 *de octubre*
11 *octobre*

A good speaker gets people to see with their ears.

৪০০৪

Un buen orador consigue que su audiencia vea con sus oídos.

৪০০৪

Un bon orateur obtient que son audience voit avec les oreilles.

ARAB PROVERB
PROVERBIO ARABE
PROVERBE ARABE

To know certain things well, learning them is not enough . . .

෫ාඥ

Hay ciertas cosas que, para saberlas bien, no basta con haberlas aprendido . . .

෫ාඥ

Pour bien connaître certaines choses, il ne suffit pas de les avoir apprises . . .

LUCIUS ANNAEUS SENECA (c. 4 B.C-c. 65 A.D.)

Roman Philosopher
Filósofo Romano
Philosophe romain

October 13
13 de octubre
13 octobre

Let a man radically alter his thoughts, and he will be astonished at the rapid transformation it will effect in the material conditions of his life. Men imagine that thought can be kept secret, but it cannot; it rapidly crystallizes into habit, and habit solidifies into circumstance.

ଓଞ

Cuando un hombre altera radicalmente sus pensamientos, queda sorprendido ante la rápida transformación que se produce en las condiciones materiales de su vida. El hombre cree que puede mantener ocultos sus pensamientos. Imposible. El pensamiento cristaliza rápidamente en hábito y el hábito se materializa en circunstancia.

ଓଞ

Qu'un homme change radicalement ses pensées et il sera étonné de la rapide transformation des conditions matérielles de son existence. On s'imagine qu'une pensée peut rester secrète. Impossible. Elle se transforme rapidement en habitudes et l'habitude devient routine.

JAMES ALLEN (1864-1912)

English Writer, Author of the book *As a Man Thinketh*
Escritor Inglés, Autor del libro *As a Man Thinketh*
Écrivain anglais, auteur du livre *As a Man Thinketh*

October 14
14 de octubre
14 octobre

How can you conceive a political system with only one party in a country that produces more than two hundred varieties of cheese!

෨෬

¡Cómo puede uno concebir un sistema político con un partido único en un país que tiene más de doscientas variedades de queso!

෨෬

Comment peut-on concevoir un système politique à parti unique dans un pays qui produit plus de deux cent variétés de fromages!

CHARLES DE GAULLE (1890-1970)

French Soldier, Writer & Statesman
Soldado, Escritor & Hombre de Estado Francés
Soldat, écrivain et homme d'État français

October 15
15 de octubre
15 octobre

The hidden place of a lie is never deep.

☙✠❧

El hoyo donde se esconde una mentira nunca es profundo.

☙✠❧

Le cachette d'un mensonge n'est jamais profonde.

Haitian Creole: "Trou manti pa fon"

HAITIAN PROVERB
PROVERBIO HAITIANO
PROVERBE HAITIEN

There is nothing stranger to man than himself. If he wants to know this stranger, he has to enter into the workshop he has inside him and close the door. There he will meet his most dangerous enemy, and he will learn to master him. He will also meet his true self, his most loyal friend, his wisest master, his most reliable counselor: HIMSELF.

ಬಂಡ

No hay nadie más extraño al hombre que él mismo. Si él quiere conocer a este extraño, que entre en su taller de trabajo y cierre la puerta. Ahí encontrará su más peligroso enemigo y aprenderá a dominarlo. Ahí encontrará, también, su verdadero yo, su amigo más fiel, su maestro más sabio, su consejero más seguro: EL MISMO.

ಬಂಡ

Rien n'est plus étranger à l'homme que lui-même. S'il veut connaître cet étranger, il doit entrer dans cet atelier qu'il a en lui-même et fermer la porte. Là, il rencontrera son ennemi le plus dangereux et apprendra à le maîtriser. Là il apprendra aussi à mieux se connaître et découvrira son ami le plus fidèle, son maître le plus sage, son conseiller le plus digne de confiance: LUI-MÊME.

BAIRD THOMAS SPALDING III (1857-1953)

English Engineer & World Traveller
Ingeniero & Viajero Universal Inglés
Ingénieur et voyageur universel anglais

October 17
17 de octubre
17 octobre

The mission of these great minds is to guide mankind over the sea of errors to the haven of truth, to draw it forth from the abysses of barbarous vulgarity up into the light of culture and refinement.

෨෦෬

La misión de estas grandes mentes es de guiar la humanidad sobre el océano de errores hacia el puerto de la verdad, de sacarla de los abismos de la bárbara vulgaridad y llevarla a la luz de la cultura y del refinamiento.

෨෦෬

La mission des grands esprits est de guider l'humanité sur l'océan des erreurs vers le havre de la vérité, de la soustraire des profondeurs de la vulgarité barbare pour la conduire vers la lumière de la culture et du raffinement.

ARTHUR SCHOPENHAUER (1788-1860)

German Philosopher
Filósofo Alemán
Philosophe allemand

October 18
18 de octubre
18 octobre

Great minds have always been confronted with the fierce opposition of mediocre minds.

୫୦ଠଃ

Las grandes mentes siempre son confrontadas con la tenaz oposición de las mentes mediocres.

୫୦ଠଃ

Les grands esprits ont toujours rencontré l'opposition violente des esprits médiocres.

ANONYMOUS
ANONIMO
ANONYME

October 19
19 de octubre
19 octobre

He who wants to change will always find a reason to do so.

୫୬

El que quiere cambiar siempre encontrará una razón para hacerlo .

୫୬

Celui qui veut vraiment changer trouvera toujours une bonne raison de le faire.

ANDRÉ MAUROIS (1885-1967)

French Writer
Escritor Francés
Écrivain français

October 20
20 de octubre
20 octobre

"I have a dream . . .
that one day on the red hills of Georgia,
sons of former slaves and sons of former slave-owners
will be able to sit down together at the table of brotherhood.
I have a dream . . .
my four children will one day live in a nation where they will not be
judged by the color of their skin but by the content of their character.
I have a dream today!"

࿓

"Tengo un sueño . . .
un día en las rojas colinas de Georgia,
los hijos de los antiguos esclavos y los hijos de sus antiguos
amos, podrán sentarse juntos en la mesa de la hermandad.
Tengo un sueño . . .
mis cuatro hijos vivirán en un país en el cual no serán juzgados
por el color de su piel, sino por los rasgos de su personalidad.
¡Hoy tengo un sueño!"

࿓

"J'ai un rêve . . .
un jour, sur les rouges collines de Georgie,
les fils des anciens esclaves et les fils de leurs anciens
maîtres pourront s'asseoir ensemble à la table de la fraternité.
J'ai un rêve . . .
Un jour, mes quatre enfants vivront dans un pays où ils ne
seront pas classés d'après la couleur de leur peau mais d'après
leur valeur personnelle.
Aujourd' hui j'ai un rêve!"

MARTIN LUTHER KING JR. (1929-1968)

American Civil Rights Leader
Líder Americano de los Derechos Civiles
Leader américain des Droits Civils

October 21
21 de octubre
21 octobre

You start getting old when you stop learning.

ಬಂದ

Uno empieza a envejecer cuando para de aprender.

ಬಂದ

On commence à vieillir quand on cesse d'apprendre.

JAPANESE PROVERB
PROVERBIO JAPONES
PROVERBE JAPONAIS

Nobody has sufficient memory to lie successfully always.

৪০৫৪

Nadie tiene la memoria suficiente para mentir siempre con éxito.

৪০৫৪

Personne n'a assez de mémoire pour se permettre de mentir avec succès à tous les coups.

ABRAHAM LINCOLN (1809-1865)

16th President of the United States of America
16° Presidente de los Estados Unidos de América
16ᵉ Président des Etats-Unis d'Amérique

Stay in front of the door if you want it opened. Don't leave the road if you want to find a guide. Nothing is closed forever except in your own eyes.

‍ 80C3

Permanezca frente a la puerta si quieres que te la abran. No abandones el camino si tú quieres conseguir un guía. Nada está cerrado por siempre excepto en tus propios ojos.

‍ 80C3

Reste devant la porte si tu veux qu'elle s'ouvre. Ne quitte pas la route si tu veux qu'on te guide. Rien n'est fermé à jamais, sauf à tes propres yeux.

FARID AL-DIN 'ATTAR (c. 1150-c. 1220)

Persian Poet
Poeta Persa
Poète perse

October 24
24 de octubre
24 octobre

I have stopped being a nightingale to become a woodpecker.

࿇

Paré de ser ruiseñor para convertirme en pájaro carpintero.

࿇

J'ai cessé d'être un rossignol pour devenir un pivert.

ERNESTO RAMOS ANTONINI (1898-1963)

Puerto Rican Politician
Prócer Puertorriqueño
Politicien portoricain

Learning is like the horizon, it has no limits.

৪৩৫৪

El aprendizaje es como el horizonte, no tiene límites.

৪৩৫৪

Apprendre est comme l'horizon, c'est-a-dire sans limites.

CHINESE PROVERB
PROVERBIO CHINO
PROVERBE CHINOIS

October 26
26 de octubre
26 octobre

It seems to me that my most outstanding achievements were realized when I had the greatest limitations in terms of Time, Money and Space.

ಚಿ CG

Me parece que las obras más extraordinarias de mi carrera fueron realizadas cuando tuve las mayores limitaciones en término de Tiempo, Dinero y Espacio.

ಚಿ CG

Il me semble que j'ai réalisé les oeuvres les plus importantes de ma carrière quand le Temps, l'Argent et l'Espace me manquaient le plus.

FRANK LLOYD WRIGHT (1869-1959)

American Architect
Arquitecto Americano
Architecte américain

October 27
27 de octubre
27 octobre

On your way to the future, weave yourself the sail of your boat, strong and tough; God will add His breeze.

&OC&

En el camino a tu futuro, haz tú mismo la vela de tu barca fuerte y robusta; Dios te compensará con Su brisa.

&OC&

En route pour la vie, tisse toi-même la voile de ta barque solide et robuste. Dieu fournira Sa brise.

JOSE C. DUARTE DA SILVEIRA (b. 1934)

Consul of Portugal in Puerto Rico
Cónsul de Portugal en Puerto Rico
Consul du Portugal à Porto Rico

The ideals which have lighted me on my way time and time again and have given me new courage to face life cheerfully, have been Truth, Goodness and Beauty.

೫೦೮೩

Los ideales que han iluminado mi camino una y otra vez y que me han dado la valentía de encarar la vida con alegría, han sido la Verdad, la Bondad y la Belleza.

೫೦೮೩

Les idéaux qui ont maintes fois illuminé mon chemin et qui ont souvent renouvelé mon courage pour faire face à la vie avec joie, ont été la Vérité, la Bonté et la Beauté.

ALBERT EINSTEIN (1879-1955)

German-born American Scientist
Científico Americano Nacido en Alemania
Scientifique américain originaire d'Allemagne

October 29
29 de octubre
29 octobre

Let me tell you the secret of my success: the source of my strength is exclusively perseverance.

૪૭૯

Déjeme decirle el secreto que me ha llevado al logro de mi meta: mi fuerza reside exclusivamente en mi tenacidad.

૪૭૯

Laissez-moi vous dire le secret qui m'a conduit à mon but: ma force se trouve exclusivement dans ma ténacité.

LOUIS PASTEUR (1822-1895)

French Chemist & Biologist
Químico & Biólogo Francés
Chimiste et biologiste français

Ask, and it shall be given you;
Seek, and ye shall find;
Knock, and it shall be opened unto you.

ℰℭ

Pidan y se les dará;
Busquen y hallarán;
Llamen a la puerta y les abrirán.

ℰℭ

Demandez et vous recevrez;
Cherchez et vous trouverez;
Frappez et on vous ouvrira.

THE BIBLE – LA BIBLIA – LA BIBLE

St. Matthew 7:7
San Mateo 7:7
St. Matthieu 7:7

October 31
31 de octubre
31 octobre

I know little, but of the little I know, I know a lot.

೫෮೦෬

Yo sé poco, pero de lo poco que sé, sé mucho.

೫෮೦෬

Je sais peu de choses, mais du peu que je sais, je sais beaucoup.

PREMIER MALDONADO (b. 1933)

Puerto Rican Conceptualist
Conceptualizador Puertorriqueño
Conceptualisateur portoricain

NOVEMBER — NOVIEMBRE — NOVEMBRE

1 ....ARISTOTLE
2 ....WILLIAM HALE WHITE
                  (MARK RUTHERFORD)
3 ....ROBERT BROWNING

4 ....EMMELINE PARKHURST
5 ....EDOUARD F. LAFONTANT
6 ....RUDOLPH GIULIANI

7 ....BOOKER T. WASHINGTON
8 ....MORRIE SCHWARTZ
9 ....THE KORAN

10 ....THE BIBLE
11 ....CHUCK YEAGER
12 ....BARUCH SPINOZA

13 ....MARCELINO CANINO SALGADO
14 ....MOTHER THERESA OF CALCUTTA
15 ....FRANçOIS MARIE AROUET — dit
                  VOLTAIRE

16 ....ANTOINE DE SAINT-EXUPÉRY
17 ............................MAKSIMOVITCH GORKI
18 ....NELSON ROLINHLAHLA MANDELA

19 ....CONFUCIUS
20 ....THOMAS ALVA EDISON
21 ....PAUL J. MEYER

22 ....JOHN F. KENNEDY
23 ....MARTIN LUTHER KING JR.
24 ....HARRISON FORD

25 ....NADINE STAIRS
26 ....ALEKSANDER SOLZHENITSYN
27 ....ANAXAGORE

28 ....MICHAEL JOHNSON
29 ....EFRAÍN TIRADO
30 ....JAMES ALLEN

The difference between an educated and uneducated man is the same difference as between being alive and being dead.

৪০ৎৡ

La diferencia entre una persona educada y una sin educación es la misma que existe entre estar vivo o estar muerto.

৪০ৎৡ

La différence entre une personne éduquée et une autre qui ne l'est pas est la même qui existe entre un être vivant et un être mort.

ARISTOTLE (384-322 B.C.)

Greek Philosopher
Filósofo Griego
Philosophe grec

Blessed are those who heal us from our low self-esteem. Of all the services available to people, I don't know of any that might be more precious.

❧

Benditos sean los que nos curan de nuestro desprecio hacia nosotros mismos. De todos los servicios que se ofrecen al ser humano, yo no conozco ninguno que para mí sea más valioso.

❧

Bénis soient ceux qui nous guérissent d'une médiocre image de nous-mêmes. De tous les services que l'on peut rendre à l'homme, je n'en connais pas de plus précieux.

WILLIAM HALE WHITE (MARK RUTHERFORD) (1831-1913)

British Writer
Escritor Inglés
Écrivain anglais

A man's reach should exceed his grasp, else what's a heaven for?

໖ၯ໙

El deseo de un hombre debería exceder lo que puede alcanzar; o sino, ¿para qué está el cielo?

໖ၯ໙

Un homme doit dépasser ce qui est immédiatement à sa portée, autrement à quoi servirait un ciel?

ROBERT BROWNING (1812-1889)

English Poet
Poeta Inglés
Poète anglais

November 4
4 de noviembre
4 novembre

We women suffragists have a great mission—the greatest mission the world has ever known. It is to free half the human race and through that freedom to save the rest.

෨෬

Nosotros las sufragistas tenemos una gran misión, la misión más noble que el mundo haya jamás conocido: la de liberar la mitad de la raza humana y al hacerlo, liberaremos la otra mitad.

෨෬

Nous les suffragettes avons une noble mission, la plus noble que le monde ait jamais connue: celle de libérer la moitié du genre humain et ainsi sauver l'autre moitié.

EMMELINE PARKHURST (1858-1928)

British Suffragette, Human Rights Militant
Militante Inglesa de los Derechos Humanos
Militante anglaise des Droits humains

November 5
5 de noviembre
5 novembre

Who can still doubt the extraordinary vision of Luis Muñoz Marín as the leader of the revolution that transformed Puerto Rico in a relatively short time! He expressed this vision in those immortal words: "I am the God-chosen pamphleteer and agitator, and I march with a crowd of stars and of hungry people toward the Great Dawn."

ॐ◌ॐ

¡Quién puede dudar que Luis Muñoz Marín tuvo una visión extraordinaria para liderear la revolución que transformó a Puerto Rico en un lapso de tiempo relativamente corto! El lo expresó en estas inmortales palabras: "Yo soy el panfletista de Dios, el agitador de Dios y ando con una turba de estrellas y de hombres hambrientos hacia la Gran Aurora."

ॐ◌ॐ

Qui peut encore douter de la vision extraordinaire de Luis Muñoz Marín le leader de la révolution qui a transformé Puerto Rico en un laps de temps relativement court? Il a exprimé cette vision par ces paroles immortelles: "Je suis le pamphlétaire choisi par Dieu, l'agitateur choisi par Dieu et j'avance avec une tourbe d'étoiles et de gens affamés vers la Grande Aurore."

EDOUARD F. LAFONTANT (b. 1932)

Master Motivator
Maestro Motivador
Maître motivateur

I spent my first seven years as Mayor living out my father's advice that it's better to be respected than loved. But I had forgotten the last part of what he used to say: "Eventually, you will love me."

80C8

He pasado mis primeros siete años como Alcalde viviendo el consejo de mi padre: es mejor ser respetado que ser querido. Pero he olvidado la última parte de lo que solía decir "y eventualmente, usted va a quererme".

80C8

Durant mes premières années comme Maire de New York, j'ai suivi ce conseil de mon père: "Vaut mieux être respecté que d'être aimé." Cependant, j'en avais oublié la dernière partie de son avertissement: "Eventuellement, vous m'aimerez."

RUDOLPH W. GIULIANI (b. 1944)

Mayor of New York, Person of the Year 2001
Alcalde de Nueva York, Hombre del Año 2001
Maire de New York, Personne de l'Année 2001

November 7
7 de noviembre
7 novembre

I have learned that success is to be measured not so much by the position that one has reached in life but by the obstacles one has overcome while trying to succeed.

଼ଓଔଓ

He aprendido que el éxito debe medirse no tanto por la posición que uno ha alcanzado en la vida como por los obstáculos que uno ha superado al intentar triunfar.

଼ଓଔଓ

J'ai appris que la réussite ne se mesure pas à l'importance de la position que l'on occupe dans la vie mais à l'étendue des obstacles franchis pour y parvenir.

BOOKER T. WASHINGTON (1856-1915)

American Educator, Founder of Tuskegee Institute
Educador Americano, Fundador del Instituto Tuskegee
Éducateur américain, fondateur de l'Institut Tuskegee

A meaningful life: Devote yourself to loving others, devote yourself to your community around you and devote yourself to creating something that gives to your life purpose and meaning.

৪০৫৪

Una vida meritoria: Dedícate a amar a los demás, dedícate a tu comunidad, y dedícate a crear algo que dará un propósito y un sentido a tu vida.

৪০৫৪

Une vie bien remplie: Aimez vos semblables, dévouez-vous au service de votre communauté et consacrez vos efforts à la création de quelque chose qui donne un sens et un but à votre vie.

MORRIE SCHWARTZ

American University Professor
From the Book *Tuesdays with Morrie*
Catedrático Universitario Americano
Professeur américain d' université

November 9
9 de noviembre
9 novembre

A good word is like a good tree whose roots are strong and whose branches try to reach the sky. It gives fruits every season.

೭೦೦೮

Una buena palabra es como un buen árbol cuyas raíces son fuertes y sus ramas alcanzan el cielo. Dá sus frutos en cada estación.

೭೦೦೮

Une bonne parole est comme un arbre fertile dont les racines sont fortes et dont les branches tendent vers le ciel. Il donne des fruits à chaque saison.

THE KORAN
EL CORAN
LE CORAN

I can do all things through Christ who strengthens me.

ಏಂಲ

Todo lo puedo en Aquel que me fortalece.

ಏಂಲ

Je peux tout par le Christ qui me fortifie.

THE BIBLE — LA BIBLIA — LA BIBLE

Philippians 4:13
Filipenses 4:13
Philippéens 4:13

November 11
11 de noviembre
11 novembre

There is no such thing as a natural born pilot. Whatever my aptitudes or talents, becoming a proficient test pilot was hard work.

৪৩০৪৩

En la naturaleza no existe tal cosa como un piloto nato. Todas mis habilidades y talentos que he desarrollado para convertirme en un piloto competente se lograron al trabajar duro para conseguirlos.

৪৩০৪৩

On ne naît pas pilote. Quels que soient mes aptitudes et mes talents, je suis devenu un pilote d'essai compétent uniquement par un travail assidu.

CHUCK YEAGER (b. 1923)

United States Air Force Test Pilot
(The first person to exceed the speed of sound in flight — 1947)
Piloto de Prueba, Fuerzas Aéreas de los Estados Unidos de América
Pilote d'essai des Forces aériennes des États-Unis d'Amérique

Our soul, being able to perceive truth, is a part of the infinite intelligence of God.

৪৩৪৪

Nuestra alma, al poder percibir la verdad, es una parte de la inteligencia infinita de Dios.

৪৩৪৪

Par sa capacité de percevoir la verité, notre esprit est une partie de l'intelligence infinie de Dieu.

BARUCH SPINOZA (1632-1677)

Dutch Philosopher
Filósofo Holandés
Philosophe hollandais

November 13
13 de noviembre
13 novembre

The abuse of power is not a corollary of power. Those who abuse it are already corrupt. Saying that power corrupts, is accepting that the fever is in the sheet.

೮೧ೞ

Quienes abusan del poder no es como consecuencia del poder intrínsicamente, sino porque ellos mismos ya son corruptos en sí. Decir que el poder corrompe es aceptar que la calentura está en la sábana.

೮೧ೞ

L'abus du pouvoir n'est pas un corollaire du pouvoir. Ceux qui en font un mauvais usage sont déjà corrompus. Dire que le pouvoir corrompt, c'est croire que c'est le drap qui cause la fièvre.

MARCELINO CANINO SALGADO

Professor at the University of Puerto Rico
Catedrático de la Universidad de Puerto Rico
Professeur à l'Université de Porto Rico

I am a little pencil in the hand of a writing God, who is sending a love letter to the world.

༄༅

Yo soy un pequeño lápiz en la mano de un Dios que escribe una carta de amor al mundo.

༄༅

Je suis un petit crayon dans la main d'un Dieu qui écrit une lettre d'amour à l'humanité.

AGNES GONXHA BOJAXHIU (1910-1997)

Mother Theresa of Calcutta
Madre Teresa de Calcuta
Mère Teresa de Calcutta

November 15
15 de noviembre
15 novembre

I did some good; it's my best accomplishment.

৪০০৪

He hecho un poco de bien; es mi mejor obra.

৪০০৪

J'ai fait un peu de bien; c'est mon meilleur ouvrage.

FRANçOIS MARIE AROUET – dit VOLTAIRE (1694-1778)

French Writer
Escritor Francés
Écrivain français

Love does not consist of gazing at each other but of looking together in the same direction.

ᏵᏨᏟᏃ

Amar, no es mirar uno al otro, es mirar los dos en la misma dirección.

ᏵᏨᏟᏃ

Aimer, ce n'est pas se regarder l'un l'autre, c'est regarder ensemble dans la même direction.

ANTOINE DE SAINT-EXUPÉRY (1900-1944)

French Aviator & Writer
Aviador & Escritor Francés
Aviateur et écrivain français

November 17
17 de noviembre
17 novembre

What a beautiful profession it is to be a man on earth!

ഇരു

¡Qué profesión más bella ser un hombre sobre la faz de la tierra!

ഇരു

Quel beau métier que d'être un homme sur la terre!

MAKSIMOVITCH GORKI (1868-1936)

Russian Writer
Escritor Ruso
Écrivain russe

Our deepest fear is not that we are inadequate.
Our deepest fear is that we are powerful beyond measure.
It is our light, not our darkness, that frighten us.
We ask ourselves, who am I to be brilliant, gorgeous, talented and fabulous?
Actually, who are you not to be?
You are a child of God.
Your playing small doesn't serve the world.
There's nothing enlightened about shrinking so that other people won't feel unsure around you.
We were born to manifest the glory of God within us.
It's not just in some of us; it's in everyone.
And as we let our own light shine, we consciously give other people permission to do the same.
As we are liberated from our own fear, our presence automatically liberates others.

NELSON ROLINHLAHLA MANDELA (b. 1918)

President, Republic of South Africa
1994 Inaugural Speech

Nuestro miedo más profundo no es que no seamos adecuados; nuestro miedo más profundo es que no hay límites a nuestro poder.

Es nuestra brillantez, no nuestro obscurantismo, lo que nos asusta.

Nos preguntamos:

¿Quién soy yo para ser tan brillante, tan hermoso, talentoso y fabuloso?

En realidad, ¿quién es usted para no poseer todas estas cualidades?

Usted es un hijo de Dios.

Al verse pequeño, en nada ayuda usted al mundo.

Usted no inspira a nadie al disminuirse para que los que le rodean se sientan más seguros.

Nacimos para manifestar la Gloria de Dios en nosotros.

No es solamente en algunos de nosotros sino en todos nosotros.

Y al dejar brillar nuestra propia luz, conscientemente permitimos a los otros a hacer lo mismo.

Al liberarnos de nuestro propio miedo,

Enseguida nuestra presencia libera a los demás.

NELSON ROLINHLAHLA MANDELA (b. 1918)

Presidente de la República de Sur Africa
1994 Discurso Inaugural

Notre souci majeur n'est pas notre incompétence,
mais notre potentiel illimité.
C'est notre rayonnement et non notre obscurantisme qui nous
inquiète. Nous nous demandons:
Qui suis-je pour être si brillant, si beau, si talenteux, si
exceptionnel?
En somme, pourquoi en serait-il autrement?
Vous êtes des enfants de Dieu.
En feignant l'humilité, on ne rend aucun service à l'humanité.
En se faisant petit pour mettre son entourage à l'aise,
On ne lui inspire rien.
Nous avons été créés pour faire resplendir la gloire de Dieu
Qui se trouve en nous.
Non pas en quelques-uns d'entre nous, mais en nous tous.
Quand nous laissons rayonner notre lumière, nous invitons
naturellement les autres à en faire autant.
Quand nous nous débarrassons de notre peur, notre présence
spontanément libère l'esprit de ceux qui nous entourent.

NELSON ROLINHLAHLA MANDELA (b. 1918)

Président de la République de l'Afrique du Sud
1994 Discours Inaugural

The true gentleman does not preach what he practices till he has practiced what he preaches.

ႚჂႩ

Un hombre verdaderamente honesto no predica sus principios hasta que él no los haya practicado.

ႚჂႩ

Un homme de bien ne prêche pas ses principes tant qu'il ne les a pas encore mis en pratique.

CONFUCIUS (c. 551-479 B.C.)

Chinese Philosopher
Filósofo Chino
Philosophe chinois

Genius is one percent inspiration and ninety-nine percent perspiration.

ഐരു

El genio es uno porciento de inspiración y noventa y nueve porciento de transpiración.

ഐരു

Le génie est un pour cent d'inspiration et quatre-vingt-dix-neuf pour cent de transpiration.

THOMAS ALVA EDISON (1847-1931)

American Inventor
Inventor Americano
Inventeur américain

Self-confidence can be gained only through practical know-how; know-how comes from knowledge and experience, and experience can be gleaned only through a willingness to confront obstacles and situations that others ordinarily fear.

৪১০৪৪

La única forma de tener confianza en sí mismo es por medio de un conocimiento práctico; éste proviene de la información y la experiencia, y esta última se recaba sólo gracias a la buena disposición para enfrentarse a los obstáculos y situaciones que las personas temen en general.

৪১০৪৪

La confiance en soi est uniquement le fruit de l'habileté. L'habileté résulte de la connaissance et de l'expérience; l'expérience s'acquiert par la détermination à faire face aux obstacles et aux situations que la majorité des gens craignent.

PAUL J. MEYER (b. 1928)

American Entrepreneur & Educator
Founder of The Success Motivation Institute's Companies
Empresario & Educador Americano
Fundador de las Empresas Success Motivation Institute
Homme d'affaires et éducateur américain
Fondateur des entreprises Success Motivation Institute

All problems are man-made and can be solved by man.

৪৩৫৪

Todos los problemas son hechos por el hombre y pueden ser resueltos por el hombre.

৪৩৫৪

Tous les problèmes sont créés par l'homme et peuvent être résolus par l'homme.

JOHN F. KENNEDY (1917-1963)

35th President of the United States of America
35[o] Presidente de los Estados Unidos de América
35e Président de États-Unis d'Amérique

When evil men plot, good men must plan. When evil men burn and bomb, good men must build and bind. When evil men shout ugly words of hatred, good men must commit themselves to the glories of love. Where evil men would seek to perpetuate an unjust status quo, good men must seek to bring into being a real order of justice.

ഇൗൽ

Cuando los hombres malos conspiran, los hombres buenos tienen que planificar. Cuando los hombres malos queman y lanzan bombas, los hombres buenos construyen y unen. Cuando los hombres malos gritan palabras feas de odio, los hombres buenos se comprometen a las glorias del amor. Cuando los hombres malos buscan perpetuar las condiciones actuales e injustas, los hombres buenos buscan realizar una condición real de justicia.

ഇൗൽ

Quand les méchants conspirent, les hommes de bien doivent planifier. Quand les méchants incendient et lancent des bombes, les hommes de bien doivent construire et s'unir. Quand les méchants prêchent la haine, les hommes de bien doivent glorifier l'amour. Là où les méchants voudraient perpétuer un statu quo injuste, les hommes de bien doivent lutter pour créer une société de droit.

MARTIN LUTHER KING JR. (1929-1968)

American Civil Rights Leader
Líder de Derechos Civiles Americano
Leader américain des Droits civils

Everybody grows up with a vision of paradise in his head.

❧☙

Cada persona crece con una visión del paraíso en su mente.

❧☙

Chacun grandit avec une vision du paradis dans la tête.

HARRISON FORD (b. 1942)

American Actor
Actor Americano
Acteur américain

If I had my life to live over . . .
I'd dare to make more mistakes next time.
I'd relax
I would limber up
I would be sillier than I have been this trip
I would take fewer things seriously
I would take more chances
I would take more trips
I would climb more mountains and swim more rivers
I would eat more ice cream and less beans.
I would perhaps have more actual troubles,
but I'd have fewer imaginary ones.
You see, I'm one of those people who live sensibly and sanely
hour after hour, day after day.
Oh! I've had my moments
and if I had it to do over again
I would have more of them.
In fact, I'd try to have nothing else.
Just moments, one after another,
instead of living so many years ahead each day.
I've been one of those persons who never goes anywhere
without a thermometer,
a hot water bottle,
a raincoat,
and a parachute.
If I had to do it again, I would travel lighter than I have.
If I had my life to live over
I would start barefoot earlier in the spring
and stay that way later in the fall.
I would go to more dances.
I would ride more merry-go-rounds, I would pick more daisies.
I would contemplate more sunrises
and play more with children.
If I had my life to live over . . .
but, you see I am 85 years old
death is not far away.

NADINE STAIRS (1893-?)
American Writer & Poet, *Instants*

Si pudiera vivir nuevamente mi vida . . .
En la próxima, trataría de cometer más errores,
no intentaría ser tan perfecto, me relajaría más.
Sería más tonto de lo que he sido, de hecho
tomaría muy pocas cosas con seriedad.
Sería menos higiénico.
Correría más riesgos, haría más viajes.
Contemplaría más atardeceres,
subiría más montañas, nadaría más en los ríos.
Iría a más lugares adonde nunca he ido,
Comería más helados y menos habas.
Tendría más problemas reales y menos imaginarios.
Yo fuí una de esas personas que vivió
sensata y prolíficamente cada minuto
de su vida; claro que tuve momentos de alegría.
Pero si pudiera volver atrás trataría
de tener más de estos buenos momentos.
Por si no lo saben, de eso está hecha
la vida, sólo de momentos, no te pierdas el ahora.
Yo era uno de esos que nunca iban a ninguna
parte sin un termómetro, una bolsa de agua
caliente, un paraguas y un paracaídas;
si pudiera volver a vivir, viajaría más liviano.
Si pudiera volver a vivir comenzaría a andar
descalzo a principios de la primavera y
seguiría así hasta concluir el otoño.
Iría a bailar más a menudo.
Daría más vueltas a caballitos,
recogería más margaritas,
contemplaría más amaneceres
y jugaría más con niños.
Si tuviera otra vez la vida por delante . . .
Pero ya ven, tengo 85 años y sé
que la muerte no está lejos.

NADINE STAIRS (1893-?)
Escritora & Poeta Americana, *Instantes*

25 novembre

Si je pouvais recommencer ma vie,
Je tâcherais de commettre davantage d'erreurs.
Je n'essayerais pas d'être parfaite,
je serais plus détendue.
Je serais un peu naïve et prendrais peu de choses au sérieux.
L'hygiène serait le cadet de mes soucis.
Je prendrais plus de risques et voyagerais davantage.
Je contemplerais plus souvent les couchers de soleil.
Je ferais l'ascencion d'un plus grand nombre de montagnes
et nagerais dans un plus grand nombre de rivières.
J'irais, autant que possible, explorer les terres qui me sont
inconnues.
Je mangerais plus de glaces et moins de fèves,
J'aurais plus de vrais problèmes et moins de problèmes
imaginaires.
J'ai été ce genre d'individu sérieux pour qui
Chaque minute de la vie doit être féconde;
Oui , j'ai connu des moments heureux,
mais si je pouvais recommencer,
J'essayerais de ne connaître que des moments heureux.
Pour votre gouverne, la vie est faite de moments,
Profitez du moment présent.
J'ai été du nombre de ceux qui ne se déplacent
Jamais sans un thermomètre, sans une gourde
d'eau fraîche, sans un parapluie et sans un parachute.
Si je pouvais recommencer, je voyagerais avec peu de bagages.
Si je pouvais recommencer, je commecerais à marcher pieds nus
plus tôt au printemps et continuerais jusqu'à la fin de
l'automne.
J'irais danser plus souvent,
je cueillerais plus de marguerites,
je jouirais davantage des manèges
Je contemplerais plus de levers de soleil
Et jouerais plus souvent avec les enfants.

Si je pouvais recommencer...
Mais j'ai déjà 85 ans et je sais que
Je ne suis pas loin de mourir.

NADINE STAIRS (1893-?)
Écrivaine et poète américaine, *Instants*

November 26
26 de noviembre
26 novembre

It is not the level of prosperity that makes for happiness but the kinship of heart to heart and the way we look at the world. Both attitudes are within our power, so that a man is happy so long as he chooses to be happy, and no one can stop him.

ഓരു

No es el nivel de prosperidad que produce la felicidad, son las relaciones afectivas y la manera de ver al mundo. Estas dos actitudes están dentro de nosotros, así un hombre es feliz si escoge ser feliz; nadie puede impedir que sea así.

ഓരു

Ce n'est pas l'argent qui fait le bonheur mais plutôt nos relations affectives et notre vision du monde. Ces deux options nous sont accesibles; ainsi, un homme est heureux tant qu'il choisit de l'être et nul ne peut l'en empêcher.

ALEKSANDER SOLZHENITSYN (b. 1918)

Russian Writer
Escritor Ruso
Écrivain russe

The visible opens our mind to the invisible.

ဆာ

Lo visible abre nuestras miradas hacia lo invisible.

ဆာ

Le visible ouvre nos regards sur l'invisible.

ANAXAGORE (c. 500-428 B.C.)

Greek Philosopher
Filósofo Griego
Philosophe grec

November 28
28 de noviembre
28 novembre

Those who said you cannot do this or that should not interrupt those who are doing it.

ഓരുൽ

Los que dicen que no se puede hacer tal o cual cosa no deben interrumpir a los que lo están haciendo.

ഓരുൽ

Les esprits négatifs ne doivent pas intervenir quand les esprits positifs agissent.

MICHAEL JOHNSON (b. 1967)

American Athlete
Atleta Americano
Athlète américain

We hear very often this popular saying: "It's better to have a million friends than a million dollars." I think that it is better to have both.

෮෧෬

Muchas veces escuchamos este popular refrán: 'Es mejor tener un millón de amigos que un millón de dólares.' Pienso que realmente lo mejor sería tener las dos cosas.

෮෧෬

On entend souvent ce proverbe: 'Il vaut mieux posséder un million d'amis qu'un million de dollars.' Je pense qu'il est préférable d'avoir les deux.

EFRAÍN TIRADO (b. 1941)

Puerto Rican Entrepreneur
Hombre de Negocios Puertorriqueño
Homme d'affaires portoricain

November 30
30 de noviembre
30 novembre

Dream lofty dreams and, as you dream, so shall you become. Your vision is the promise of what you shall one day be; your ideal is the prophecy of what you shall at last unveil.

ഃൠരു

Tenga sueños sublimes y usted llegará a ser como sus sueños. Su visión será la promesa de lo que un día será; su ideal será el augurio de lo que al fin descubrirá.

ഃൠരു

Ayez toujours des rêves sublimes car vous deviendrez ce que vous rêvez d'être. Votre vision est le prélude de votre avenir; votre idéal est la prophétie de vos réalisations.

JAMES ALLEN (1864-1912)

English Writer, Author of the book *As a Man Thinketh*
Escritor Inglés, Autor del libro *As a Man Thinketh*
Écrivain anglais, auteur du livre *As a Man Thinketh*

DECEMBER – DICIEMBRE – DÉCEMBRE

1 . . . . .EDOUARD F. LAFONTANT
2 . . . . .MARTIN LUTHER KING JR.
3 . . . . .CARLOS GHOSN

4 . . . . .ANDRÉ MALRAUX
5 . . . . .JEAN-JACQUES ROUSSEAU
6 . . . . .HAN YU

7 . . . . .NORMAN VINCENT PEALE
8 . . . . .EDOUARD F. LAFONTANT
9 . . . . .JOHN D. ROCKEFELLER

10 . . . . .MOHONDAS "MAHATMA" GANDHI
11 . . . . .VICTOR HUGO
12 . . . . .MOTHER THERESA OF CALCUTTA

13 . . . . .THOMAS J. WATSON SR.
14 . . . . .GEORGE SANTAYANA
15 . . . . .AMARTYA SEN

16 . . . . .HENRIK IBSEN
17 . . . . .JOHN M. CAPOZZI
18 . . . . .CLAUDE ADRIAN HELVETIUS

19 . . . . .DONNA OLIVER
20 . . . . .TURKISH PROVERB
21 . . . . .DALAI LAMA

22 . . . . .JAMES ALLEN
23 . . . . .TOSHIWO DOKO
24 . . . . .RAISSA MARITAIN

25 . . . . .ANONYMOUS
26 . . . . .PABLO CASALS
27 . . . . .JACK WELCH

28 . . . . .LEOPOLDO GÓMEZ
29 . . . . .PAUL J. MEYER
30 . . . . .MARK D. SANDERS & TIA SILLERS
31 . . . . .PLOTINUS

December 1
1 de diciembre
1ᵉʳ décembre

After reading the adventures of Tim Whittaker and Eric Weihenmayer climbing to the top of Mount Everest — the former a cripple without legs, the latter blind — I concluded that every human being whether crippled without legs or blind should choose his own Everest to climb.

৪৩৪৪

Después de leer las hazañas de Tim Whittaker y de Eric Weihenmayer - al subir al tope del Monte Everest, el primero sin piernas y el otro sin ojos - creo que cada ser humano debería escoger su propio Everest para subir aunque sea lisiado o ciego.

৪৩৪৪

Aprés avoir lu les exploits de Tim Whittaker et de Eric Weinhenmayer qui ont escaladé le Mont Everest, le premier cul-de-jatte, l'autre aveugle, j'ai conclu que chaque être humain devrait choisir son propre Mont Everest, quelle que soit son infirmité.

EDOUARD F. LAFONTANT (b. 1932)

Master Motivator
Maestro Motivador
Maître motivateur

One day we will learn that the heart can never be totally right if the head is totally wrong. Only through bringing together the head and the heart—intelligence and goodness—shall man rise to the fulfillment of his true nature.

ഇൗങ

Un día aprenderemos que el corazón nunca puede ser totalmente correcto si la cabeza es totalmente incorrecta. Solamente al armonizar cabeza y corazón - inteligencia y bondad - que el ser humano podrá elevarse a la realización de su verdadera naturaleza.

ഇൗങ

Un jour nous apprendrons que le coeur et la tête doivent fonctionner en parfaite harmonie. C'est seulement en unissant la tête et le coeur, intelligence et bonté, que l'homme pourra s'élever à la hauteur de sa vraie nature.

MARTIN LUTHER KING JR. (1929-1968)

American Civil Rights Leader
Líder Americano de Derechos Civiles
Leader américain des Droits civils

Nationalities are not exclusive. You are not only what it says on your passport. National culture is additive . . . I belong to many countries, many environments. I find myself comfortable in Beirut (Lebanon), Greenville (South Carolina), Tokyo, Paris, and Rio de Janeiro. You simply add from one national culture to another. The more you add, the more you balance.

ഇൗരു

Las nacionalidades no son exclusivas. Usted no es solamente lo que está escrito en su pasaporte. La cultura nacional es aditiva. Pertenezco a muchos países, muchos ambientes. Me siento cómodo en Beirut (Líbano), en Greenville (Carolina del Sur), en Tokyo, Paris y Rio de Janeiro. Simplemente uno suma una cultura nacional sobre la otra. Cuanto más culturas se suman, mayor es su satisfacción.

ഇൗരു

Les nationalités ne sont pas exclusives. Vous n'êtes pas seulement ce qui est inscrit sur votre passeport. La culture nationale est cumulative . . . J'appartiens à beaucoup de pays et de milieux. Je me sens également à l'aise à Beyrouth (Liban), à Greenville (Caroline du Sud), à Tokyo, à Paris, ou à Rio de Janeiro. Tout simplement, vous cumulez les cultures nationales; plus vous en ajoutez, plus vous vous sentez à l'aise dans le monde.

CARLOS GHOSN (b. 1954)

CEO of Nissan Corp. (Japan)
[Turn Around — How Carlos Ghosn Rescued Nissan by David Magee]
PDG de Nissan Corp.
PDG de la Nissan Corp.

The history of art is the history of mankind.

ଓୱେଷ

La historia del arte es la historia del hombre.

ଓୱେଷ

L'histoire de l'art est l'histoire de l'Homme.

ANDRÉ MALRAUX (1901-1976)

French Writer
Escritor Francés
Écrivain français

December 5
5 de diciembre
5 décembre

To renounce liberty is to renounce being a man, to surrender the fights of humanity and even to fail one's duties.

ఴఴ

Renunciar a la libertad es renunciar a ser hombre, es abandonar las luchas de la humanidad y hasta olvidar sus obligaciones.

ఴఴ

Renier la liberté c'est renoncer à être un homme, c'est capituler dans les combats de l'humanité et même faillir à ses devoirs.

JEAN-JACQUES ROUSSEAU (1712-1778)

French Writer & Philosopher
Escritor & Filósofo Francés
Écrivain et philosophe français

He who sits at the bottom of a well to contemplate the sky will find it small.

೮౦౧౩

El cielo le parecerá muy pequeño al que se sienta en el fondo de un pozo para contemplarlo.

೮౦౧౩

Celui qui s'assied au fond d'un puits pour contempler le ciel le trouvera petit.

HAN YU (768-824)

Chinese Writer
Escritor Chino
Écrivain chinois

December 7
7 de diciembre
7 décembre

You can permit obstacles to control your mind to the point where they are uppermost and thus becoming the dominating factors in your thought pattern. By learning how to cast them from the mind, by refusing to become mentally subservient to them, and by chanelling spiritual power through your thoughts you can rise above obstacles which ordinarily might defeat you.

❧☙

Usted puede dejar que unos obstáculos controlen su mente al extremo de convertirse en los factores predominantes de su forma de pensar. Al aprender como arrojar estos obstáculos de su mente, al no dejarse dominar por ellos y al canalizar el poder espiritual en sus pensamientos, usted puede elevarse por encima de estos obstáculos que podrían eventualmente derrotarlo.

❧☙

Vous pouvez permettre aux difficultés de contrôler votre cerveau au point qu'elles deviennent les facteurs essentiels et dominants de votre mode de penser. Cependant, en apprenant à les écarter de votre esprit, en refusant d'être leur prisonnier et en laissant le pouvoir de l'esprit guider votre pensée, vous pouvez surmonter les difficultés qui ordinairement vous paralysent.

NORMAN VINCENT PEALE (1898-1993)

American Clergyman & Author
Clérigo & Escritor Americano
Ministre protestant et écrivain américain

If success is the progressive realization of important, predetermined, personal and worthwhile goals, here is an effective formula to live a life of continuous success according to Aristotle's thought:

$$Q (i + e + m) = s^n$$

Intelectual quotient + emotional quotient + moral quotient

= unlimited success.

୫୦୯୫

Si el éxito es la realización progresiva de metas importantes, predeterminadas, personales y meritorias, a la luz del pensamiento de Aristóteles, he aquí una fórmula práctica para vivir una vida de éxito contínuo:

$$C (i + e + m) = e^n$$

Cociente intelectual + cociente emocional + cociente moral

= Éxito ilimitado

୫୦୯୫

Si la réussite est la réalisation progressive de buts importants, prédéterminés, personnels et valables, nous pouvons selon Aristote établir la formule suivante pour une vie de réussites:

$$Q (i + e + m) = r^n$$

Quotient intellectuel + quotient émotionnel + quotient moral

= réussite illimitée

EDOUARD F. LAFONTANT (b. 1932)

Master Motivator
Maestro Motivador
Maître motivateur

The moment to be happy is now.
The place to be happy is here.
The way to be happy is to act.

❧☙

El momento de ser feliz es ahora.
El lugar de ser feliz es aquí.
La manera de ser feliz es hacer.

❧☙

Le moment pour être heureux c'est maintenant.
Le lieu pour être heureux c'est ici.
Le moyen d'être heureux c'est l'action.

JOHN D. ROCKEFELLER (1839-1937)

American Entrepreneur
Industrial Americano
Industriel américain

Every night when I go to sleep, I die. Next morning, when I awake, I am born again.

৪০০৪

Cada noche, cuando voy a dormir, me muero. Y al día siguiente, cuando me despierto, nazco de nuevo.

৪০০৪

Chaque soir, quand je vais dormir, je meurs. Le lendemain à mon réveil, je renais.

MOHONDAS "MAHATMA" GANDHI (1869-1948)

Indian Political & Religious Leader
Líder Político & Religioso Indio
Leader politique et religieux indien

December 11
11 *de diciembre*
11 *décembre*

My coat and myself live together in perfect harmony; it hides my wrinkles; it does not hurt me anywhere and has molded itself to my imperfections; it does not impair my movements; I only feel its presence because it keeps me warm. An old friend is like an old coat.

৪০৫৪

Mi abrigo y yo vivimos juntos cómodamente. Ha asumido todas mis arrugas, ya no me molesta en parte alguna, se ha moldeado a mis deformidades. Se muestra complaciente con todos mis movimientos y sólo siento su presencia porque me mantiene caliente. Un viejo amigo es como un viejo abrigo.

৪০৫৪

Mon manteau et moi vivons ensemble en parfaite harmonie. Il cache mes rides et ne me fait mal en aucun endroit; il épouse gentiment les imperfections de mon corps et ne gêne pas mes mouvements. Je ne ressens sa présence que parce qu'il me tient chaud. Un vieil ami, c'est tout comme un vieux manteau.

VICTOR HUGO (1802-1885)

French Writer
Escritor Francés
Écrivain français

If you are kind, people will accuse you of selfish motives . . .
So be kind anyway.
If you are successful, you will win both false and true enemies . . .
Succeed anyway.
What you spend years building, someone may destroy
overnight . . .
Build anyway.
The good you do today most people forget . . .
So do good anyway.
Give the world the best you have, and it may not be enough . . .
Give your best anyway.
In the final analysis… it's between you and God . . .
It never was between you and them anyway!!!

AGNES GONXHA BOJAXHIU (1910-1997)

Mother Theresa of Calcutta
(Quote received from a dear friend, Ian Frederics of New Zealand)

Si usted es amable, la gente lo acusará de tener motivos
egoístas . . .
Aún así, sea amable.
Si usted es exitoso, ganará falsos y verdaderos enemigos . . .
Aún así, sea exitoso.
Lo que le ha costado años construir, alguien podrá destruirlo . . .
Aún así, siga construyendo.
El bien que usted hace hoy, lo olvidará la mayoría de la gente . . .
Aún así, sigue haciendo el bien.
Dé lo mejor de usted al mundo, y posiblemente no será
suficiente . . .
Aún así, siga dando lo mejor de usted.
En resumidas cuentas . . . es un asunto entre usted y Dios . . .
De todos modos nunca ha sido un asunto entre usted y los demás.

AGNES GONXHA BOJAXHIU (1910-1997)

Madre Teresa de Calcuta
(Recibido de un buen amigo Ian Frederics de New Zealand)

Si vous êtes aimable, les gens vous accuseront d'avoir des
intentions égoïstes . . .
Soyez aimable quand même.
Si vous réussissez, votre succès vous créera de faux et de vrais
ennemis . . .
Poursuivez quand même la réussite.
En une nuit quelqu'un peut détruire ce que vous avez mis de
longues années à construire . . .
Continuez quand même à construire.
La plupart des gens oublieront le bien que vous faites
aujourd'hui . . .
Continuez quand même à faire du bien.
Donnez au monde le meilleur de vous-même, probablement ce
ne sera pas assez . . .
Continuez à donner le meilleur de vous-même.
En fin de compte, il s'agit d'une affaire entre vous et Dieu . . .
De toute façon ce ne fut jamais une affaire entre vous et les autres.

AGNES GONXHA BOJAXHIU (1910-1997)

Mère Teresa de Calcutta
(Reçu d'un bon ami Ian Frederics de Nouvelle-Zélande)

December 13
13 de diciembre
13 décembre

If you want to increase your success rate, don't be afraid to increase your failure rate.

৪০৫৪

Si usted quiere aumentar su taza de éxito, aumente su taza de fracasos.

৪০৫৪

Si vous voulez augmenter votre taux de réussite, ne craignez pas d'augmenter votre taux d'échecs.

THOMAS J. WATSON SR. (1874-1956)

American Entrepreneur, Founder of IBM
Empresario Americano, Fundador de IBM
Homme d'affaires américain, Fondateur de IBM

There is no remedy for birth and death, except the enjoyment of the interlapse.

୫୬ଓଷ

No hay remedio para el nacimiento y la muerte, salvo disfrutar del intervalo.

୫୬ଓଷ

On n'a aucun contrôle sur la naissance et sur la mort, alors profitons de l'entre-temps.

GEORGE SANTAYANA (1863-1952)

American Philosopher, Poet & Humanist
Filósofo, Poeta & Humanista Americano
Philosophe, poète et humaniste américain

December 15
15 diciembre
15 décembre

The countries that will be ahead in the 21st Century are those who invest in education and health.

∞∞

Los países que se mantendrán a la vanguardia en el siglo 21° serán aquellos que inviertan en la educación y la salud del país.

∞∞

Les pays qui seront à l'avant-garde au 21e siècle sont ceux qui investissent dans l'éducation et la santé.

AMARTYA SEN

Nobel Prize Winner in Economy
Premio Nobel en Economía
Prix Nobel d' économie

A community is like a ship, everyone ought to be prepared to take the helm.

୫୦ଓଓ

Una comunidad es como un barco, todos deben estar preparados para tomar el timón.

୫୦ଓଓ

Une communauté est comme un bateau, chacun doit être prêt à prendre le gouvernail.

HENRIK IBSEN (1828-1906)

Norwegian Writer
Escritor Noruego
Écrivain norvégien

December 17
17 de diciembre
17 décembre

Even if the entire Board of Directors votes for a dumb idea, it's still a dumb idea.

ഇൗരു

Aún cuando todos los miembros de la Junta de Directores voten por una idea estúpida, sigue siendo una idea estúpida.

ഇൗരു

Même si tous les membres d'un conseil d'administration votent pour une idée stupide, cette idée demeure stupide.

JOHN M. CAPOZZI

American Airlines Executive
Un Dirigente de la American Airlines
Un dirigeant de la American Airlines

An individual without passions has within himself neither principle of action, nor motive to act. By suppressing the desires, you suppress the mind.

৩৩৫৪

Cada persona que no tenga pasión dentro de él tampoco tiene principio de acción ni motivo para actuar. Al anular los deseos, se anula también la mente.

৩৩৫৪

Un individu sans passion dans le cœur n'a ni plan d'action, ni raison pour agir. La supression des désirs entraîne celle de l'esprit.

CLAUDE ADRIEN HELVETIUS (1715-1771)

French Philosopher
Filósofo Francés
Philosophe français

December 19
19 *de diciembre*
19 *décembre*

Teachers are the architectural designers of nations. People must see that education is not an expense but an investment.

ᏸᏜᏣ

Los maestros son los arquitectos de las naciones. Debemos aceptar que la educación no es un gasto sino una inversión.

ᏸᏜᏣ

Les enseignants sont les architectes des nations. On doit comprendre que l'éducation n'est pas une dépense mais un investissement.

DONNA OLIVER

1987 United States of America's Teacher of the Year
Maestra del Año 1987 de los Estados Unidos de América
Professeur de l'année 1987 aux État-Unis d'Amérique

December 20
20 de diciembre
20 décembre

Through failures we learn to win.

&⊃&

Los fracasos son los cimientos de la victoria.

&⊃&

C'est par les échecs que nous apprenons à vaincre.

TURKISH PROVERB
PROVERBIO TURCO
PROVERBE TURC

December 21
21 de diciembre
21 décembre

I would like to be able to transform myself anytime, now and always,
into a protector for those who do not have protection,
into a guide for those who are lost,
into a boat for those who want to cross the ocean,
into a bridge for those who have to cross a river,
into a sanctuary for those who are in danger,
into a lamp for those who are in the dark,
into a place of refuge for those who do not have a shelter,
into a servant for those in need.

೫೦೪೫

Quisiera poder convertirme en cualquier momento ahora y siempre,
en un protector de los que no tienen protección,
en un guía para los que están perdidos,
en un barco para los que quieren cruzar los oceános,
en un puente para los que tienen un río que cruzar,
en un santuario para los que están en peligro,
en una lámpara para los que andan en la obscuridad,
en un lugar de refugio para los que no tienen un techo,
en un servidor para los necesitados.

೫೦೪೫

Je voudrais pouvoir me transformer en tout moment
maintenant et toujours
en un protecteur pour ceux qui n'ont pas de protection,
en un guide pour les égarés,
en un bateau pour ceux qui veulent traverser les océans,
en un pont pour ceux qui doivent traverser une rivière,
en un sanctuaire pour ceux qui sont en danger,
en une lumière pour ceux qui vivent dans l'obscurité,
en un toit pour les sans logis,
en un serviteur pour les nécessiteux.

TENZIN GYATSO, 14th DALAI LAMA (b. 1935)

Spiritual Leader of Tibet
Líder Espiritual del Tibet
Leader spirituel du Tibet

In all human affairs there are efforts and there are results, and the strength of the effort is the measure of the result. Chance is not. Gifts, powers, material, intellectual and spiritual possessions are the fruits of effort; they are thoughts completed, objects accomplished, visions realized. The vision that you glorify in your mind, the ideal that you enthrone in your heart—this you will build your life by; this you will become.

෨෧

En todo el acontecer humano hay esfuerzos y hay resultados y la grandeza del esfuerzo dará la medida del resultado. No existe la suerte. Los dones, los poderes, las posesiones materiales, intelectuales y espirituales son frutos del esfuerzo; son pensamientos que han sido completados, son objetivos cumplidos, son sueños hechos realidad. La imagen que usted exalta en su mente, el ideal que entroniza en su corazón - será lo que le dé la pauta – para construir su vida, será aquello en lo que usted se convertirá.

෨෧

Dans toute enterprise humaine, il y a des efforts et des résultats et le résultat est proportionnel à la puissance de l'effort. Le facteur chance n'intervient pas. Les dons, les pouvoirs, les possessions matérielles, intellectuelles et spirituelles sont les fruits de l'effort; ce sont des idées concrétisées, des objectifs atteints, des visions réalisées. La vision que vous glorifiez dans votre esprit, l'idéal que vous couronnez dans votre coeur, voilà ce sur quoi vous allez bâtir votre vie, voilà ce que vous allez devenir.

JAMES ALLEN (1864-1912)
English Writer, Author of the book *As a Man Thinketh*
Escritor Inglés, Autor del libro *As a Man Thinketh*
Écrivain anglais, auteur du livre *As a Man Thinketh*

December 23
23 de diciembre
23 décembre

We have no natural resource. We have no military might. We only have one resource: the inventive capacity of our brains. This capacity is unlimited. We have to develop it. We have to educate ourselves, to train, to equip ourselves. This mental power will finally become in a near future the most precious common treasure of all mankind.

ଈୠଓଔ

Nosotros no tenemos ningún recurso natural, ningún poderío militar. Sólo tenemos un recurso: la capacidad de invención de nuestros cerebros. Esta es ilimitada. Hay que desarrollarla. Hay que educar, adiestrar, equipar. Esta potencia cerebral llegará a ser, por la fuerza de las cosas, en un futuro próximo, el bien común más precioso y más creador de la humanidad entera.

ଈୠଓଔ

Nous autres japonais n'avons ni ressources naturelles, ni puissance militaire. Nous ne possédons qu'une seule source de richesses: la matière grise, celle-là illimitée. Pour l'exploiter, nous devons nous éduquer, nous entraîner et nous équiper. Dans un proche avenir, cette matière grise sera universellement considérée comme la richesse commune la plus précieuse de toute l'humanité.

TOSHIWO DOKO

President of Keindanren: National Federation of Japanese Industries
Presidente de Keindanren: Federación Nacional de Industrias Japonesas
Président du Keindanren: Fédération nationale des Industries japonaises

December 24
24 de diciembre
24 décembre

All men are made from the same clay, but not from the same breath.

ଈଓଔଓ

Todos los hombres son hechos del mismo barro, pero no del mismo soplo.

ଈଓଔଓ

Tous les hommes sont faits du même limon, mais pas du même souffle.

RAISSA MARITAIN

Diary of French Philosopher Jacques Maritain
Diario del Filósofo Francés Jacques Maritain
Carnet de notes du philosophe français Jacques Maritain

December 25

ONE SOLITARY LIFE

He was born in an obscure village, the child of a peasant woman. He grew up in another village, where He worked in a carpenter shop until He was thirty. Then for three years He was an itinerant preacher.

He was a defender of unpopular causes. He counted among His friends the poor and the weak. He associated with outcasts and lawbreakers.

He never wrote a book. He never held an office. He never had a family or owned a house. He didn't go to college. He never traveled more than two hundred miles from the place of His birth. He had no credential but Himself.

He was only thirty-three when the tide of public opinion turned against Him. His friends ran away. He was turned over to His enemies and went through the mockery of a trial. He was spat on, flogged and ridiculed and was nailed to a cross between two thieves. While He was dying, His executioners gambled for His clothing, the only property He had on earth. When He was dead, He was laid in a borrowed grave through the pity of a friend.

Nearly 2,000 years have come and gone, and today He is the central figure of the human race and the leader of mankind's progress.

All the armies that ever marched, all the navies that ever sailed, all the parliaments that ever sat, all the kings that ever reigned, all these together, have not affected the life of man on this earth as much as that: **ONE SOLITARY LIFE**.

ANONYMOUS

UNA VIDA SOLITARIA

Nació en una humilde aldea, hijo de una campesina. Creció en otra pequeña aldea donde trabajó en un taller de carpintería hasta los treinta años. Durante los tres años siguientes, fue un predicador itinerante.

Fue el defensor de las causas poco comunes. Era amigo de los pobres y desvalidos y compartía con rebeldes y delincuentes.

Nunca escribió un libro. Nunca tuvo una oficina. Nunca se casó ni fue dueño de una casa. No asistió a la universidad. Nunca viajó más allá de 200 millas de su lugar de nacimiento. Sus únicas credenciales fueron Él mismo.

Tenía solamente 33 años cuando las corrientes de la opinión pública se pusieron en contra de Él. Sus amigos lo abandonaron. Él fue entregado a sus enemigos y tuvo que sufrir las burlas en un juicio injusto. Fue escupido, flagelado, ridiculizado, crucificado y puesto entre dos ladrones. Mientras agonizaba, sus verdugos se rifaron sus ropas, lo único que tenía en la tierra. Cuando murió fue sepultado en una tumba provista por la generosidad de un amigo.

Han pasado 2000 años y hoy Él es la figura central de la raza humana y el líder del progreso de la humanidad.

Todos los ejércitos que han marchado, todas las armadas que han navegado, todos los parlamentos que se han constituido, todos los reyes que han reinado, todos juntos, no han afectado la vida del ser humano en la tierra como lo ha hecho esta: **VIDA SOLITARIA**.

ANONIMO

UNE VIE SOLITAIRE

Né dans un petit village, fils d'une paysanne, Il a grandi dans un autre petit village voisin où Il travailla comme charpentier jusqu'à l'âge de trente ans. Durant les trois années qui suivirent Il a été un prédicateur itinérant.

Il était le défenseur des causes perdues. Il était l'ami des pauvres et des marginaux, Il fréquentait aussi des rebelles et des hors-la-loi.

Il n'a jamais écrit un livre, n'a jamais eu un bureau. Il n'a jamais fondé une famille, n'a jamais possédé une maison. Il n'a jamais fréquenté l'université. Il n'a jamais voyagé plus loin qu'a 200 milles de sa ville natale. Sa seule richesse était sa personne.

Il avait seulement trente trois ans quand la marée de l'opinion publique s'est retournée contre lui. Abandonné par ses amis, Il a été livré à ses ennemies et exposé aux moqueries des autres lors de son jugement. Ils ont craché sur son visage, Ils l'ont flagellé, Ils l'ont ridiculisé et Ils l'ont crucifié entre deux voleurs. Tandis qu'il agonisait, ses bourreaux ont tiré au sort sa tunique, l'unique bien qu'Il possédait sur terre. Quand Il mourut, sa dépouille a été déposée dans un tombeau grâce à la générosité d'un ami.

2000 ans se sont écoulés. Aujourd'hui encore Il demeure le personnage principal de la race humaine et le leader par excellence des progrès de l'humanité.

Toutes les armées qui ont défilé, toutes les flottes qui ont navigué, tous les parlements qui ont siégé, et tous les rois qui ont régné sur terre, mis ensemble n'ont pas eu autant d'influence sur la vie de l'être humain que cette: **VIE SOLITAIRE**.

ANONYME

Every day, every minute, every dawn, every flower, every drop of the sea—this sea linked with mine, far away, but always there—convinced me that life is a miracle and every one a marvel that we should maintain with our effort, our faith and our love. For this reason, the same day of my 96th birthday, the first thing I did was to give a big hug to mother nature and then do my piano and cello routine. After that, I could start my day. Today I still believe the same and for this reason, I want to send to all this message: Never stop to work for what you desire; life is an endless discovery, and we have to comply.

ഇരുള

Cada día, cada minuto, cada amanecer, cada flor, cada gota del mar - de ese mar que se enlaza con el mío, lejos, pero presente - me hacen sentir más identificado con la idea de que vivir es un milagro y de que todos y cada uno de nosotros somos una maravilla que nunca terminamos de pagar con nuestro esfuerzo, con nuestra fe, con nuestro amor. Por eso, el mismo día que cumplía noventa y seis años, lo primero que hice fue abrazarme a la naturaleza y luego trabajar en mi piano y en mi violoncello. Después de eso, ya todo podía comenzar. Y hoy creo lo mismo y por eso quiero enviar a todos este mensaje: No dejéis nunca de trabajar por lo que deseáis; la vida es un descubrimiento constante y hay que cumplir con él.

ഇരുള

Chaque jour, chaque minute, chaque aurore, chaque fleur, chaque goutte de la mer, cette mer qui enlace celle de ma patrie lointaine mais toujours présente, renforce ma conviction que la vie est un miracle et chaque individu une merveille que nous ne devons jamais cesser d'entretenir par notre travail, notre confiance en l'avenir et notre amour. Ainsi, le jour de mes quatre vingt seize ans, mon premier geste, après avoir embrassé la nature, fut de pratiquer mon piano et mon violoncelle. Ensuite, j'ai commencé ma journée. Aujourd'hui ma conviction n'a pas changé; c'est pourquoi je veux envoyer ce message à vous tous: Ne cessez jamais de travailler à la réalisation de vos rêves. La vie est une découverte permanente, on doit s'y conformer.

PABLO CASALS (1876-1973)

Spanish Musician & Composer
Músico & Compositor Español
Musicien et compositeur espagnol

Change before it's too late.

৪ও৫৪

Cambia antes de que sea demasiado tarde.

৪ও৫৪

Changez avant qu'il ne soit trop tard.

JACK WELCH
CEO General Electric Corp.

From the book *Get Better or Get Beaten*
Del Libro *Get Better or Get Beaten*
Du livre *Get Better or Get Beaten*

December 28
28 de diciembre
28 décembre

Above the clouds, the sky is always blue.

୨୦୦ଓ

Encima de la nubes, el cielo sigue siendo azul.

୨୦୦ଓ

Au dessus des nuages, le ciel est toujours bleu.

**TEXT OF A POSTCARD SENT BY MY DEAR FRIEND
LEOPOLDO GÓMEZ FROM THE DOMINICAN REPUBLIC
(1982)
TEXTO DE UNA TARJETA POSTAL ENVIADA POR MI
AMIGO LEOPOLDO GÓMEZ DE LA REPUBLICA
DOMINICANA
TEXTE D'UNE CARTE POSTALE REÇUE DE MON BON AMI
LEOPOLDO GÓMEZ DE LA REPUBLIQUE DOMINICAINE**

I'll never retire, I enjoy working
to do all the good necessary,
by all the means I can,
in all the ways I can,
in all the places I can,
to all the people I can, as long as I live.

෨൚ଓ

Nunca me jubilaré, disfruto de mi trabajo
para hacer todo el bien necesario,
por todos los medios posibles,
en todas las maneras posibles,
en todos los lugares posibles,
a todas las personas a mi alcance, hasta mi último suspiro.

෨൚ଓ

Je ne prendrai jamais ma retraite,
j'aime travailler pour répandre le bien,
par tous les moyens en mon pouvoir,
de toutes les manières possibles,
dans tous les endroits accessibles,
à tous les humains, tant qu'il me restera un souffle de vie.

PAUL J. MEYER (b. 1928)

American Entrepreneur & Educator
Founder of The Success Motivation Institute's Companies
Empresario & Educador Americano
Fundador de las Empresas Success Motivation Institute
Homme d'affaires et éducateur américain
Fondateur des entreprises Success Motivation Institute

. . . You can bottle youth.
What you store in it is up to you.
(I suggest your heart).
If you can figure out a way to keep
the energy and gumption and fire alive,
you will always stay young.
And where there's youth, there's hope . . .
Where there's hope, there's wonder . . .
Where there's wonder, there's faith . . .
Where there's faith, there's chance . . .
Where there's chance, there's love . . .
Where there's love, there's music . . . and dancing.
I hope you dance; I really hope you dance.

MARK D. SANDERS & TIA SILLERS

Authors of *I Hope You Dance*

. . . Tú puedes embotellar tu juventud.
Lo que guardes en tu botella depende de ti.
(Sugiero tu corazón).
Si puedes imaginarte una manera de mantener
viva tu energía, tu coraje y tu pasión,
siempre serás joven.
Y donde hay juventud, hay esperanza . . .
Donde hay esperanza, hay asombro . . .
Donde hay asombro, hay fe . . .
Donde hay fe, hay suerte . . .
Donde hay suerte, hay amor . . .
Donde hay amor, hay música . . . y baile.
Espero que bailes; de verdad espero que bailes.

MARK D. SANDERS & TIA SILLERS

Autores de *I Hope You Dance*

Vous pouvez mettre votre jeunesse en bouteille.
Ce que vous y mettez dépend de vous.
(Je suggère votre coeur).
Si vous pouvez trouver un moyen de garder en vie
votre énergie, votre courage et votre enthousiasme,
vous resterez toujours jeune.
Car, là où il y a la jeunesse, il y a espoir . . .
Là où il y a l'espoir, il y a surprise . . .
Là où il y a la surprise, il y a foi . . .
Là où il y a la foi, il y a chance . . .
Là où il y a la chance, il y a amour . . .
Là où il y a l'amour, il y a musique et danse . . .
Je vous souhaite de danser;
Sincèrement je vous souhaite de danser.

MARK D. SANDERS & TIA SILLERS

Auteurs de *I Hope You Dance*

Don't stop carving your own statue until it reveals the divine splendor of your talents.

                                    ಔಚ

No pares de esculpir tu propia estatua hasta que te revele el esplendor divino de tus talentos.

                                    ಔಚ

N'arrête pas de sculpter ta propre statue tant qu'elle ne t'aura pas révélé la divine splendeur de tes talents.

PLOTINUS (c. 205-c. 270 A.D.)

Alexandrian Philosopher
Filósofo Alejandrino
Philosophe alexandrine

ALPHABETIC INDEX OF AUTHORS

Adams, Donald A.	04/14
Adams, Henry Brooks	01/23
Addison, Joseph	10/10
Adenauer, Konrad	01/20
Adler, Mortimer J.	01/04, 03/21, 04/30
Advertising by Nissan Motors	10/09
African Legend	07/01
Albizu Campos, Pedro	08/27
Al-Din Áttar, Farid	10/23
Alelon, Mary	04/08
Allen, James	01/08, 02/17, 03/31, 04/25, 05/24, 09/24, 10/13, 11/30, 12/22
An American Glassblower	10/05
Anaxagore	11/27
Annan, Kofi	09/30
Anonymous	03/23, 03/25, 03/26, 04/09, 04/15, 04/16, 04/27, 05/06, 05/23, 06/29, 07/16, 07/27, 08/10, 09/10, 10/18, 12/25
Aristotle	11/01
Aurelius, Marcus Antoninus	02/20, 08/21
Baba, Sai	05/28
Bach, Richard	05/25
Baird, David	09/28
Ball, Lucille	09/13

Barnes, Emilie	08/11
Benítez, Jaime	08/31
Bergson, Henri	04/21
Better Business Bureau	07/21
Bible, The	01/12, 02/16, 03/12, 05/26, 06/01, 07/25, 08/20, 09/15, 10/30, 11/10
Blake, William	04/12
Bolívar, Simón	05/21
Bonaparte, Napoléon	06/15
Borges, Jorge Luis	02/29
Braun, Wernher Von	04/04
Browning, Robert	11/03
Burke, Edmond	07/26
Busia, Akousa	02/27
Callimachus	02/09
Camus, Albert	02/13, 03/20, 05/02
Canino Salgado, Marcelino	11/13
Capozzi, John M.	08/14, 12/17
Carrel, Alexis	07/29
Casals, Pablo	02/23, 08/03, 12/26
Cervantes, Miguel de	07/06, 10/07
Chanel, Gabrielle "Coco"	07/14
Churchill, Winston	07/30
Cicero	04/20
Clark, Ramsey	02/03
Confucius	09/18, 11/19
Conrad, Joseph	08/05

Dalai Lama	05/05, 06/19, 12/21
Da Vinci, Leonardo	01/16
De Gaulle, Charles	08/18, 10/14
De Hostos, Eugenio María	01/11, 04/29
De La Cruz, San Juan	01/06
Deming, W. Edward	02/26
De St. Éxupéry, Antoine	01/13, 11/16
De Unamuno, Miguel	09/16
Dickens, Charles	08/09
Disraeli, Benjamin	06/22
Doko, Toshiwo	12/23
Donne, John	10/01
Doyle, Arthur Conan	07/27
Duarte Da Silveira, José	10/27
Duprée, Max	07/03
Edison, Thomas A.	11/20
Einstein, Albert	06/13, 10/28
Emerson, Ralph Waldo	01/02, 03/03, 05/31, 06/17
Ferré, Luis A.	02/19, 08/23, 09/08
Ferré, Sor Isolina	03/09
Ford, Harrison	11/24
Ford, Henry	02/21, 03/14, 05/18, 06/27, 07/18
Frankl, Victor Emil	01/03
Franklin, Benjamin	06/06, 07/17
Fromm, Eric	05/29
Galileo, Galilei	8/16
Gandhi, Indira	4/10

Gandhi, Mohondas "Mahatma"	05/19, 06/28, 07/02, 12/10
Gere, Richard	05/04
Ghosn, Carlos	12/03
Gide, André	08/22
Giuliani, Rudolph	11/06
Goethe, Johann Wolfgang	03/16, 04/13, 05/10, 07/13, 08/12, 09/20
Gómez, Leopoldo	12/28
Gorki, Maksimovitch	09/21, 11/17
Green, Graham	08/15
Gregory, Dick	04/28
Greig, Nordohl	08/29
Guevara, Ernesto "Che"	06/14
Haberman, Martin	09/12
Hahn, Kurt	02/07
Hegel, Friedrich	04/26
Helvetius, Claude Adrian	12/18
Henderson Brit, Steuart	04/19
Heraclitus	01/25, 03/07
Ho Chi Minh	03/29
Holmes, Oliver Wendell	02/25, 07/31
Horatius, Quintus Flacus	09/27
Hugo, Victor	01/05, 05/14, 06/30, 07/22, 08/06, 12/11
Huttinot Lafontant, Simone	02/11
Ibsen, Henrik	12/16
Jefferson, Thomas	01/30, 02/28, 06/23
Jelloun, Tahar Ben	08/25

Johnson, Michael	11/28
Johnson, Samuel	06/26
Jonson, Ben	07/10
Jordan, Vernon	03/28
Joyce, James	06/12
Jung, Carl Gustav	03/15
Kant, Immanuel	03/06
Kafka, Franz	01/29
Kazantzakis, Nikos	08/07
Keller, Helen Adams	03/08, 07/11
Kennedy, John F.	03/10, 11/22
King, Martin Luther Jr.	01/15, 05/15, 10/20, 11/23, 12/02
Koran, The	11/09
Krishnamurti, Jiddu	01/07
Kroc, Ray	02/24
Lafontaine, Jean de	07/09
Lafontant, Edouard F.	01/26, 02/12, 03/11, 04/22, 05/08, 06/11, 07/05, 08/04, 09/02, 10/02, 11/05, 12/07
Lao-Tzu	01/28
Lasorda, Tommy	09/23
Lavater, John Kaspar	06/02
Lichtenberg, Greg Christoph	09/05
Lincoln, Abraham	04/23, 06/04, 10/22
Maldonado, Alex	10/06
Maldonado, Premier	10/31

Malraux, André	04/06, 07/19, 12/04
Mandela, Nelson Rolinhlahla	11/18
Mandino, Og	06/20
Mann, Horace	03/01, 06/24
Mao Tse Tung	06/09
Maritain, Jacques	08/19
Maritain, Raissa	12/24
Martí, José	02/15, 03/17
Marx, Mother of Karl	02/04
Maugham, William Somerset	04/01, 06/25
Maurois, André	10/19
McArthur, Douglas	05/20
McLane, Drayton	03/30
McMillan, Harold	06/18
Menander	01/24, 02/10
Mendoza, Inés M.	05/07
Meng-Tse	01/17
Metchnikoff, Elie	03/05
Meyer, Paul J.	01/01, 02/06, 03/13, 04/05, 05/30, 06/10, 07/20, 08/28, 09/04, 10/08, 11/21, 12/29
Millikan, Robert	01/31
Mother Theresa of Calcutta	01/27, 11/14, 12/12
Muñoz Marín, Luis	02/18
Nehru, Jawaharlal	05/16
Neumann, Franz Ernst	08/08
Oliver, Donna	12/19

Paige, Satchel	09/07
Parker, Dorothy	01/19
Parkhurst, Emmeline	11/04
Pascal, Blaise	03/22, 06/08
Pasteur, Louis	10/29
Patton, George S.	09/26
Peale, Norman Vincent	12/07
Penney, James Cash	05/03
Pericles	09/22
Petrolini, John H.	07/15
Pirandelo, Luigi	03/04
Plato	06/03
Plotinus	12/31
Poincarré, Jules Henri	06/21
Pope John Paul II	05/22, 09/17
Powell, Colin	01/22
Premier Cruise Lines Advertising	08/13
Pressburg, Henriette	02/04
Proverb, Arab	08/24, 10/11
Proverb, Haitian	10/15
Proverb, Japanese	01/14, 10/21
Proverb, Russian	04/02
Proverb, Swedish	05/27
Proverb, Turkish	12/20
Proverb, Chinese	02/02, 04/07, 09/11, 10/25
Pythagore	06/16
Ramos Antonini, Ernesto	10/24
Ríos, Ethel de Betancourt	08/01
Robinson, Ma.	05/09
Rockefeller, John D.	08/02, 12/09
Rodin, Auguste	04/18
Rogers, Will	06/05
Roosevelt, Eleanor	01/10, 03/24
Roosevelt, Theodore	08/30
Routte Gómez, Eneid	07/12

Rousseau, Jean-Jacques	12/05
Rutherford, Mark	08/17, 11/02
Saadi, Mocharrafoddin	09/09
Santayana, George	12/14
Sanders, Mark D.	12/30
Schopenhauer, Arthur	09/03, 10/17
Schwartz, Morrie	11/08
Schweitzer, Albert	07/28
Shaprut, Hisdai Ibn	09/29
Shaw, George Bernard	05/01
Sen, Amartya	12/15
Seneca, Lucius Annae	08/26, 09/14, 10/12
Sillers, Tia	12/30
Solzhenitsyn, Alexander	11/26
Spalding, Baird T.	03/18, 10/16
Spielberg, Steven	05/12
Spinoza, Baruch	11/12
St. Evremond	03/02
Steinbeck, John	05/13
Stairs, Nadine	11/25
Stevenson, Robert L.	01/09
Swift, Johathan	09/06
Tagore, Rabindranath	10/03
Talmud	10/04
Thoreau, Henry David	04/03
Tirado, Efraín	11/29
Tolstoy, Leo	07/08
Trudeau, Pierre E.	01/21
Tutu, Desmond	02/01
Victor, Paul Emile	09/25
Virgile	03/19

Voltaire   02/05, 07/07,
                                   09/01, 11/15

Walton, Sam M.   04/24, 06/07
Ward, Lloyd David   07/23
Washington, Booker T.   01/18, 11/07
Washington, George   07/04
Watson, Thomas Jr.   04/17, 12/13
Welch, Jack   12/27
White, William Hale   08/17, 11/02
Williamson, Marianne   02/22
Wooden, John   05/17
Wright, Frank Lloyd   10/26

Yeager, Chuck   11/11
Young, Andrew   05/11
Yu, Han   12/06

Ziglar, Zig   03/27

Author Contact Information

Leadership Dynamics Institute, Inc.
Edouard F. Lafontant
1708 Santa Agueda Cupey
San Juan, Puerto Rico 00926

Phone: (787) 758-4266/4203
Fax: (787) 758-9524

E-mail: leaders@coqui.net

Edouard F. Lafontant
Master Motivator

Lo que usted tiene en sus manos es una compilación invaluable de citaciones que Edouard ha reunido desde su juventud.Peter Hein de Dinamarca dijo una vez: "Los dichos cortos a menudo abren una pequeña ventana sobre un inmenso mundo". En esta colección, filósofos, escritores, líderes cívicos, religiosos, empresariales y también Edouard abren pequeñas ventanas sobre unos inmensos mundos de satisfacción personal y de éxito profesional.

Quiero alentarlo a mantener este libro en su mesa de noche, o en su tocador. Lea la citación del día por la mañana y otra vez por la noche. Como dice un antiguo refrán nórdico: "Los proverbios parecen divertidos después de una lectura superficial pero después de reflexionar aparece el sentido más profundo". Lea estos pensamientos con mucha atención, hágalos suyos, y deje que su mente los absorba al nivel más profundo. Deje que estas verdades transformen su manera de pensar en una de optimismo, de afirmación y de motivación para reinventarse y lograr sus metas personales y profesionales.

Paul J. Meyer
Fundador de Success Motivation® International
y más de 40 empresas de la Familia Meyer

ESTE LIBRO ES IMPRESCINDIBLE PARA:

LIDERES	MEDICOS	COMERCIANTES
ESTUDIANTES	FACILITADORES	AMAS DE CASA
MAESTROS	ATLETAS	INGENIEROS
VENDEDORES	ADMINISTRADORES	CIENTIFICOS
ABOGADOS	TRABAJADORES	SUPERVISORES
ARTISTAS	CONFERENCIANTES	PADRES
EDUCADORES	ESCRITORES	PREDICADORES
POLITICOS	PSICOLOGOS	TRABAJADORES SOCIALES...

. . . y todos los que verdaderamente quieren seguir "esculpiendo su propia estatua hasta que se revele el esplendor divino de sus talentos."

Edouard F. Lafontant
Master Motivator

Ce livre que vous avez en votre possession est une sélection de pensées d'une valeur inestimable qu'Edouard n'a pas cessé de compiler depuis son adolescence. Comme a dit un penseur danois Peter Hein «Souvent de simples proverbes ouvrent une petite fenêtre sur un monde immense.» Dans cette compilation de pensées positives, des philosophes, des écrivains, des leaders politiques ou religieux, des hommes d'affaires célèbres et Edouard Lafontant lui-même ouvrent de petites fenêtres sur de vastes horizons de satisfaction personnelle et de réussites professionnelles.

Je vous encourage à faire de cet ouvrage votre livre de chevet. Lisez la pensée du jour, le matin à votre réveil et le soir avant de dormir. D'après un veil adage scandinave «Les proverbes paraissent amusants après une lecture superficielle mais profonds quand on y réfléchit.» Lisez ces pensées avec attention, prenez les à coeur et permettez à votre esprit d'en dégager la force positive et la sagesse profonde. Laissez ces vérités transformer vos réflexions en optimisme, en conviction et en motivation pour vous réinventer et atteindre les objectifs de votre vie privée et de votre carrière.

Paul J. Meyer, Fondateur de
Success Motivation® International, Inc.
et de plus de 40 Entreprises de la famille Meyer

CE LIVRE EST INCONTOURNABLE POUR:

LEADERS	MÉDECINS	COMMERçANTS
ÉTUDIANTS	FACILITATEURS	PÈRES ET MÈRES
		DE FAMILLE
ENSEIGNANTS	ATHLÈTES	INGÉNIEURS
VENDEURS	ADMINISTRATEURS	SCIENTIFIQUES
AVOCATS	OUVRIERS	SUPERVISEURS
ARTISTES	CONFÉRENCIERS	PARENTS
ÉDUCATEURS	ÉCRIVAINS	PRÉDICATEURS
HOMMES	PSYCHOLOGUES	ASSISTANTS
POLITIQUES		SOCIAUX....

. . . et tous ceux qui vraiment veulent continuer à «sculpter leur propre statue tant qu'elle n'aura pas révélé la splendeur divine de leurs talents.»